LANGUAGE AND CULTURE

Studies edited by
EMILIO PERUZZI

LINGUISTICS
and
LITERARY CRITICISM

by

GIACOMO DEVOTO

Professor of Linguistics at the University of Florence

Translated and adapted by
M. F. EDGERTON, JR.
Bucknell University

S . F . V A N N I
PUBLISHERS & BOOKSELLERS
30 WEST 12TH STREET
NEW YORK

TABLE OF CONTENTS

FOREWORD

The purpose of this book is to attempt to bring the American public into closer contact with problems and debates which are being actively pursued in Italy. The original Italian text of this present work will not be published separately. The material which it contains will form part of another book quite different from this one, which will appear in the future.

I owe this present English text, which faithfully reflects the Italian original, to the ability, patience and spirit of sacrifice of Professor Mills F. Edgerton, Jr., who has solved a number of difficult problems in an incomparable way. I should also like to thank my friend Emilio Peruzzi who originally suggested the idea for this publication. Finally, I should like to say that I have fond memories of my colleagues and students in the Department of Italian of the University of California at Berkeley, with whom I have discussed some of these problems, and to whom I wish to dedicate this book.

GIACOMO DEVOTO

TRANSLATOR'S PREFACE

It must be borne in mind by the reader of this English text that the author's Italian presents difficulties of such an order that only approximations of many of his terms are possible in English. The translator has endeavored to comment on these in the alphabetically arranged lists which follow and has included such remarks in the text itself as might facilitate the reading of it.

The translator is responsible for the English versions of the passages quoted from Italian critics and literary works, except in those cases where another source is specifically indicated. His aim has been to render into English prose the style as well as the content of the Italian original in the belief that an author is best represented to a foreign audience if the stylistic preferences of the translator do not intrude themselves into the translation.

The translator, in his rôle of adapter, has omitted from this English version only those few things contained in the Italian text which it seemed to him would necessarily be meaningless to a British or American reader lacking a thorough command of Italian language and literature. The alternative was to write a lengthy excursus in each case. With the consent of the author, therefore, such passages — few and brief, in any case — were omitted. The reader is asked to be patient and indulgent if he finds that some references are obscure in spite of the translator's efforts; his best interests are served, in any case, by the retention of as much as possible of the original work.

The translator has, of course, cited the specific Italian words and phrases with which the author deals at various points in his exposition, but to facilitate the task of the reader, whose Italian may be weak, he has usually accompanied each of them with a parenthesis containing an English equivalent and, occasionally, brief remarks of a grammatical order. It has also seemed advisable, especially in the case of Italian grammatical terminology, to place the original Italian in parentheses immediately after the term selected as a serviceable English equivalent. The English-speaking reader is presumed to have such knowledge of the basic facts of Italian literary history as will render superfluous an appendix of authors and works mentioned in the text.

When the author quotes from Italian literary texts both the original and the translator's English version are given. The Italian is retained for the benefit of those who can read it and for those whose linguistic resources are such that they will find it profitable to inspect the Italian text with the aid of the translation. In the case of critical works it has not seemed necessary to retain the original texts. In certain cases the author discusses stylistic questions which are understandable only if the reader has a knowledge of the semantics of the Italian vocabulary involved; in these cases no systematic attempt to explain the issue has been made by the translator, but, in his rôle as adapter, he has chosen to retain such passages since this present work will undoubtedly be read by many who do know Italian, and the original Italian will not have appeared in print. Nonetheless, in some cases the translator has added brief parenthetical remarks of an explanatory nature where it has seemed appropriate to do so. He and he alone is to blame for whatever omissions may be apparent in this respect.

In the case of verse, the translator has attempted to give the reader a parallel text which will, it is hoped, enable him to read the original with at least a modicum of profit, even if he knows little or no Italian. He is presumed, however, to have some knowledge of Latin, French or Spanish. Naturally, the English in these cases is not intended as an artistic version of the text; it has no other purpose than to aid the reader. A similar purpose is served by closely literal

English renderings in the case of a number of short prose passages, particularly the telegrams cited in Chapter V. *Pedagogized,* for example, is one of a lamentably long list of similarly ill-begotten words which cannot but offend the ear of the sensitive speaker of English. The translator's excuse is that no readily acceptable alternative existed, short of a complete rewriting of the passages in which they occur. Italian is, in some ways, more agile at creating and digesting new words than is English. *Juridicized* and *technified* are further examples of solutions arrived at unwillingly in similar circumstances. There are numerous other instances in the text. There are, nonetheless, limits beyond which English cannot be stretched and where those limits are reached recourse must be had to other possibilities; *epicità,* for instance, is rendered as a substantivized adjective, *the epic,* in a context in which it is readily apparent that the homonymous substantive is not intended.

ITALIAN TERMS NEEDING SPECIAL COMMENT

Antefatto.

Of all the problems this text has posed for the translator none was thornier than the need for a suitable English rendering for the substantive *antefatto.* English dictionaries do, indeed, register the word *antefact,* obviously a likely candidate, but it is archaic and rare in any sense and unknown to professional philosophers and to academicians whose special interest is literary criticism. It is, therefore, apparent that a more immediately understandable equivalent had to be found. The expression — for no single English word would bear the burden — which seemed most appropriate in all the varied contexts in which the Italian *antefatto* appeared — and the translator is of the opinion that a translation ought to represent the original as closely as proper respect for the second language will allow — is *preëxisting datum.* The reader

4

unfamiliar with the Italian term must constantly bear in mind that for the author *preëxisting datum* is a unitary concept.

Istituti.

This term has systematically been translated as *institutions;* the reader must always remember that in this case the English is semantically but an approximation of the Italian.

Lingua individuale.

This Italian term has been rendered into French as *langue individuelle,* rather than into English, since it is intended as a companion third term to the Saussurean *langue* and *parole,* and there is, therefore, no way to English it adequately.

Momento.

Occasionally the Italian *momento* and its plural *momenti* have been rendered as *momentum* and *momenta,* since these Latin forms seemed to the translator somehow better to express the author's thought.

Parola.

This term has been rendered into French, *parole,* where appropriate, since the use of the original French terms of the Saussurean terminology is standard in English, a language which offers no exact equivalents for the key terms *parole* and *langue.* The Italian *parola pregrammaticale* is similarly rendered into French as *parole prégrammaticale.*

Politica.

The Italian *politica* does the work of the English *politics* and *policy* (in certain senses) and must be rendered appropriately; the reader, however, should remember that the underlying Italian in the two cases is the same.

Pratico-empirico.

The extremely frequent Italian compounds of the type of *pratico-empirico* have been duplicated in English whenever it has been possible to do so without working undue violence on the English language; *practical-empirical* and its congeners are at least no longer outlandish in English, whether or no they must be labeled outrageous by the sensitive speaker. The translator has, in general, avoided the forms in -*o*, sometimes found in similar compounds, i.e. he has preferred *practical-empirical* to *practico-empirical*.

Realizzare, realizzazione.

The reader is cautioned that the English verb *to realize* and its derivative substantive *realization* are renderings of the Italian *realizzare* and *realizzazione* and that they uniformly have the meaning inherent in their etymology, *to make real*, etc.

Rielaborazione.

This noun has been translated as *reworking*, a choice which is certainly not beyond reproach.

Scienza, scienziato, scientifico.

The Italian substantive *scienza* retains the broad range of its Latin etymon, *scientia*, a derivative of the present participle of the verb *scire*, and is best equated with the German *Wissenschaft*. It has, however, been rendered into English as *science* and the reader should interpret this latter word accordingly. *Scienziato*, however, in this present context finds an adequate translation in the English *scholar*, in its modern academic sense. The adjective *scientifico* is the German *wissenschaftlich*; it refers to all

6

serious scholarly work of an academic nature; it has been translated as *scientific* or *scholarly*, as the context dictated.

Sociologismo.

In the *Conclusions* the translator has Anglicized the Italian *sociologismo, normativismo* and *fonetismo* as *sociologism, normativism* and *phonetism*, for lack of convenient existing equivalents. The terms refer, as the reader will readily discern, to widespread propensities of nineteenth-century philology and linguistic studies.

Spirito.

The Italian *spirito* (Latin *spiritus*) presents almost insuperable problems for the translator, since English makes use of a variety of terms, each appropriate to certain circumstances and each conveying a part of the meaning of *spirito*. The translator has made do with *mind* and *spirit* and has resisted the temptation to supply a different word except in circumstances —- and they are rare — in which neither of these terms is English.

Storia romanzata.

This term has been rendered into French as *histoire romancée* simply because English lacks a serviceable equivalent and the French term is readily understandable to the literary specialist.

ENGLISH AND FRENCH-ITALIAN INDEX

7

Parole: see *parola.*
Phonetism: see *sociologismo.*
Policy: see *politica.*
Politics: see *politica.*
Practical-empirical, et sim.: see *pratico-empirico.*
Preëxisting datum: see *antefatto.*
Realize, realization: see *realizzare.*
Reworking: see *rielaborazione.*
Science, scientific: see *scienza.*
Sociologism: see *sociologismo.*
Spirit: see *spirito.*

AUTHOR'S PREFACE

The aim of these pages is to expound in a reasonable and coherent way the relationship which exists between the two concepts of *stylistics* and *literary criticism*. They constitute a sequel to an earlier volume of mine, *Studi di stilistica* (*Studies in Stylistics*, Florence, 1950),[1] and are also related to my *Fondamenti della storia linguistica* (*Principles of Linguistic History*, Florence, 1951),[2] and to the *Profilo di storia linguistica italiana* (*Outline of Italian Linguistic History*, second edition, Florence, 1954), a work which is a first application of those *principles*.

I am reserving for a later volume the problems of the figurative arts and of their critical schemes and a comparison of these latter with the criteria usually applied to literary works.[3] Everything referring to the 'agrammatical' phase[4] of our expressive needs has been put off until that time.

And since I hope to be able to devote a later study to the history of the notion of stylistics, I have, in this present work, reduced the historical and bibliographical aspects to the indispensable minimum, limiting myself to an exposition of new points of view, debated essentially by Italian writers.

[1] Spitzer, *Spettatore italiano*, VIII (1955), pp. 356-363.

[2] Pulgram, *Language*, XXVIII (1952), pp. 261f. Hall, *Studies in Linguistics*, IX (1951), pp. 69-76. Cf. also my reply to Hall in *Lingua nostra*, XII (1951), pp. 112-114.

[3] Fubini, *Critica e poesia*, Bari, 1956, p. 118.

[4] *Fondamenti della storia linguistica*, Florence, 1951, p. 8. Cf. also Calogero, *Estetica, semantica, istorica*, Turin, 1947, and Garin, "La letteratura e le arti," *Atti del V. Congresso internazionale di lingue e letterature moderne*, Florence, 1955, pp. 3-10.

I

INTRODUCTION

I have always thought it necessary to expound scientific problems in a form acceptable to scholars of whatever philosophic,[1] as well as political or religious, persuasion. This not anti-philosophical but, rather, *a-philosophical* approach does not mean that I ignore philosophical problems. All of our reasoning tends, in fact, to free itself from the influence of instincts and passions. In order to do this, however, no debate or profession of philosophical faith is necessary. It suffices to be aware of the points of departure from which our work proceeds.

And awareness means not the certainty of being right or condemnation of those who start from other points of view, but mental clarity and careful distinction of what is taken for granted from what we are trying to demonstrate.

A consequence of this attitude is the attenuation, if not the absence, of all polemic. And, in fact, if we proceed in this way, we are not confronted by a solid, massive, doctrinal structure built stone upon stone, outside of which ERROR reigns supreme. We have, rather, a ceaseless process of creation by which a doctrine, as though it were a living organism, acquires autonomy and a personality from the fruits of other doctrines, or from accepted intuitive principles. It follows its own course, after which it is dissolved into other doctrines and attitudes, far from our immediate interest, and not destined to be the object of our attention, observation and reworking.

This work has the problems of stylistics as its principal subject. These are based on accepted concepts and crit-

---

[1] *Studi di stilistica*, Florence, 1950, pp. 8f.

ical definitions, attain maturity and a solution, and finally take the form of grammatical theories, without themselves becoming involved in grammatical debates, now extraneous to the purposes of this work.

This attitude, which is not rigid and, so to speak, remissive, is not always pleasing to the reader. To some it may seem even 'agnostic' or 'eclectic' — a rather serious accusation.

The reader is warned, therefore, that the ultimate bases of this book are those which in America are generally called 'mentalistic', and 'idealistic' in Europe. As the book progresses individual statements will often deviate from idealistic orthodoxy, and, in particular, from the doctrines of unimaginative followers of the Crocean message. Between the radical current of thought which, in the problems treated here, sacrifices all to a pan-aesthetic vision, fusing the linguistic and literary points of view, and the conservative current which is ready to jettison the aesthetic ballast on condition that the canons of historicism be saved, the present work leans toward the latter.

The scholar's task does not consist solely in concentrating his attention on the 'becoming' of things and human experiences rather than on their 'being.' It consists in drawing attention, alternately, to the creative action of individuals and to the influence of the ideals and environments which, at one and the same time, stimulate and condition that action.

Insofar as the exposition is concerned, I shall try to remain on that level of "acuity and rare intellectual agility" which I have been said to possess, as well as to keep to myself that criticism "of not comparable limpidity and constructive vigor" for which I was criticized in connection with *Studi di stilistica*.[2]

On the other hand I shall not try to establish a rigid system of terminology. But neither shall I wander about

2 By M. Sansone in *Giornale di filologia*, IV (1951), p. 193.

encumbered by an approximate terminology and, above all, I will not deprive myself of that bit of mischievous pleasure which consists in inserting into a work of 'mentalistic' inspiration technical terms and images drawn — according to some in an "annoying" way — from geometry and from the sciences of nature.

I

THE AREA

Our first task should be to define, by means of an elementary geometric image, the respective areas of stylistics and literary criticism. But, instead, we must first answer two preliminary questions: whether, in the ideal space of literary criticism and stylistics both are equally legitimately contained; and, whether, if indeed they are so contained, they occupy and exhaust all of that ideal space.

The legitimacy of literary criticism has been the object of many debates[1] but whatever the preferred formula may be to define its relationship to artistic creations, we shall assume that such a formula has been agreed upon. The legitimacy of an autonomous stylistics ought, on the other hand, to be seen to be clearly demonstrated in the pages of this present work.

The answer to the second question is, on the other hand, negative. An artistic creation, realized in literary form, obliges us to take a position on factual data and problems which are not subsumed under the pair of terms *stylistics* and *literary criticism*. A work of literary art requires of us a knowledge of the language in which it is written. It presupposes, on our part, acceptance of the conventions of the language, a knowledge of those values and oppositions which support its grammatical structure and allow us to distinguish its institutions.[2]

Grammar cannot, obviously, be absorbed into criticism or into stylistics, but it is, nevertheless, an essential factor

---

[1] For the discussions concerning the legitimacy of criticism see Fubini, op. cit., p. 3.

[2] See my *Fondamenti della storia linguistica*, cited above, pp. 26ff.

for our purposes as readers. Instead of a pair, *stylistics* and *criticism*, to be defined in their constituent elements, we find ourselves faced with the necessity of making a system of *three* pairs: *stylistics* as related to *criticism, grammar* in its relationship to *stylistics,* and *criticism's* relationship to *grammar.* We are faced with the triad *criticism, stylistics* and *grammar.*

And, since at first sight there can be no doubt concerning the respective autonomy of grammar and criticism, the problem consists in determining the possibility or legitimacy of the *insertion* of stylistics into the ample space in which criticism on the one hand and grammar on the other move without getting in each other's way, the former concentrating on the consideration of an individual realization closed within itself, perfect and, at the same time, out-dated, which is called the *parole* in the terminology of the great Swiss linguist Ferdinand de Saussure, the latter concentrating on describing a set of relationships which are collectively accepted, preëxisting and, at the same time, lasting although, naturally, not immobile, what in the same terminology constitutes the *langue.*[3]

The insertion of this third area is carried out by successive instances of trial and error. One possibility is represented by the image of a common area open to the influence of criticism on the one side and to that of grammar on the other. A parallel would be a map on which a yellowish color indicated a hilly area between the dark brown of the mountains and the green of the plain.

And, in fact, the critic cannot do without grammar and the grammarian cannot describe a language without having investigated the texts. Communication and an understanding between the two activities are indispensable; a common force seems necessarily to distinguish and, at the

---

[3] This distinction, so fundamental as to be almost Lapalissian, remains valid in spite of the objections of not only literary critics but linguists; for an example of the latter see Pulgram, loc. cit. Nevertheless, Contini's two fundamental criticisms must be borne in mind; see *Lettere di oggi,* V (1943), pp. 77-91, and *Lingua nostra,* XI (1950), pp. 51-57.

16

same time, to join together the two domains. And the name *stylistics* could be used to refer to this function of connecting the two principal areas.

The other possibility is to be seen, on the other hand, in the image of a no-man's-land which, even though it is not impossible to cross, is clearly distinct from the two main areas; as though between the brown and the green areas mentioned earlier, there were the white of a strip of desert or the blue of a body of water. Arguments in favor of this second possibility are found in philosophy.

To use the terminology from which, as we have said, this work takes its point of departure, criticism, which is aesthetic activity, is identified with one of the activities typical of the theoretical mind, while grammar is one of the activities of the practical mind. If its empirical and pedagogical character is too greatly accentuated, grammar then refers to an area which is quite marginal to the activities of the spirit. It is difficult to see how we can pass from the theoretical world of aesthetics to the practical-empirical world of grammatical pedagogy without a mediator or a shock. Criticism and grammar leave a void in this Crocean system. And since, in spite of everything, the bonds between criticism and grammar must be dealt with, this void must be filled and be named.

On the philosophical level this void may be represented by an economic and a juridical area, to which grammar corresponds only partially. On the literary and linguistic level, ours, the name that comes to mind to baptize the void is again *stylistics*.

A first approximation on our road toward the definition of stylistics and its delimitation can, therefore, be summed up as follows: stylistics corresponds to the area common to criticism and grammar; stylistics corresponds to the great area that separates criticism from grammar. These two definitions are not mutually exclusive. Whichever interpretation prevails, that arrived at by contrasting critical and grammatical relationships as opposites or the 'gradualistic'

17

interpretation, the justification for an intermediate area (desert or hills) remains.

Stylistics thus occupies a place in the great world of the practical mind and of its juridical and economic manifestations, which grammar does not exhaust.

Before going on to define those manifestations more precisely, it is indispensable to eliminate the misunderstanding of those who see something inferior and less worthy in the notion of the 'practical mind' as opposed to the theoretical mind. There is no such inferiority. To quote a scholar from among the Crocean conservatives, with whom I must often disagree, Mario Sansone, "The spirit is always industriousness, inventiveness, creation; such is also, naturally, the practical mind in its sphere, that of doing; it is not a question, as many still believe, of an activity which orders things almost blindly."[4]

For this reason even the economic and juridical world, into which we are engaged in inserting stylistics, has a concreteness of its own, even though it is different from that which is proper to the manifestations of the theoretical mind. When Mario Fubini opposes the "heuristic schemes"[5] of practical activity (which he interprets restrictively as pedagogical) to historical (theoretical) reality, he limits concreteness to pure, individual reality and arbitrarily denies the concreteness of social or collective reality, even if this latter is different and less pleasing. When he speaks of "standard" or "choice" as "concepts of comfort"[6] he does not recognize that they are both compatible with the economic and juridical world. When he denies the reality of the "average language," he ignores the fact that, in the economic and juridical sphere, there can be no language which is not collective, that is to say, average.

Those linguistic facts of which we refused to permit any individual, that is to say aesthetic analysis would cer-

4 Loc. cit., p. 211.
5 Op. cit., p. 50.
6 Op. cit., p. 49.

tainly be stripped of their intimate essence.[7] But this does not mean that along with the individual analysis we should not accept the social analysis, and with like dignity.

Still it is at this point that an objection presents itself to those who adhere to such a transplanting of the opposition between the theoretical and the practical from philosophy to the field of literature and linguistics. If on the philosophical level we have a bipartite division between theory and practice, the bipartite distinction between criticism and grammar on the linguistic level should suffice and the insertion of stylistics ought, therefore, to be superfluous.

In order to answer this objection, we must decide to what extent grammar exhausts in language what is defined in philosophy as the notion of the practical. And since the philosophical notion has been precisely defined on an earlier page by means of the pair of terms 'economic' and 'juridical' we must measure the adherence and the adaptability of the notion of grammar to these two aspects of the activity of the practical mind.

It has been repeatedly shown[8] that grammar describes standards and conventions of languages as social institutions which are quite comparable to juridical institutions. But, since it has been said[9] that there is "error" and "something deceptive" in this parallel, it must be reaffirmed that the difference between the two systems is limited to the greater grammatical importance of the juridical laws, by which the judge applies paragraphs and 'pedagogized' standards, while the language is based on custom and a much more spontaneous observance.

Nothing forbids us to imagine a language juridicized to such an extent that all freedom for the fantasy to create is taken away, as happens in the language of mathematics

[7] Op. cit., p. 344.

[8] In my *Studi di stilistica*, pp. 14f., and *Fondamenti della storia linguistica*, pp. 27ff.

[9] Loc. cit., p. 203.

19

or chemistry, in a way parallel to the police state envisioned for the technified society of the future which will take away all spontaneity in relations among citizens. And, thus, nothing prevents us from imagining a society in which a kind of 'juridical aestheticity' might continue to exist, within which 'aestheticity,' unorganized into constitutions, codices or precise legal texts, the judge would simultaneously apply and make the laws, just as the individual speaker simultaneously applies and creates linguistic relationships. We cannot imagine the grammatical crime of all those who first pronounced *oricla* instead of *auricula* against the warnings of the grammarian Probus.[10] It is a crime comparable to that of those who broke the food-supply laws of Diocletian or, in times nearer to our own, those who broke the rationing laws during the last war. Little by little *oricla* became a more popular and obvious model in relation to the more precious and rarer *auricula*, and consequently it constituted an ever more attractive possible choice. A parallel is to be found in the many legal provisions pertaining to food supplies which were not rescinded but simply fell into disuse. Finally there came a day when people said *oricla* with a feeling of certainty, through a lexical baptism which had consecrated it as the only recognized term. A parallel situation is the abandonment of rationing cards after they had been asked for in restaurants over a certain period of time with decreasing perseverance.

Inversely, the word *senex* for 'old man' once enjoyed sole recognition as, for instance, polygamy among certain peoples. Little by little *vetulus* encroached on its territory and *senex* then existed only as a left-over, fast becoming archaic, much as polygamy is going out of style. Finally, *sene*, used by Dante twice in the *Paradiso*, is a word no longer used, just as polygamy, officially prohibited, may crop up here and there.

A tripartite division is justified by these parallels. In

10 See my *Storia della lingua di Roma*, second edition, Bologna, 1944, p. 293.

20

the first series of examples, *oricla*, as a juridical crime is still on the plane of aesthetic creation; the condition of equilibrium and choice with respect to *auris* is comparable to an economic act; in its final triumph *oricla* obtains exclusive juridical recognition. Error, as creation, is still referable to literary (not necessarily poetic) creation, the choice to stylistics, and the final consecration to grammar.

In the second series the exclusive use of *senex* is a juridical and grammatical fact, the alternative use of *vetulus* and *senex* is an economic and stylistic fact and the abnormal use of *sene*, found in isolation, is an aesthetic fact.

Grammar, in the strict sense, fills only the juridical part of our economical and juridical areas; by itself it does not guarantee intimate connection with the aesthetic area. Sansone's expression[11] ought to be corrected, changed from negative to positive: "Tertium datur." But this *tertium* which is so difficult to understand, is not the result of an intermediate element, a hybrid of the theoretical and practical minds, but moves within the practical mind and does so precisely in correspondence with the 'economic' sector, (economic, naturally, in the philosophical sense), as the study of human impulses within the framework of human society.[12] It is not important to decide to what extent this implies an analogy with the aspirations of Paul Valéry.[13]

These statements, which are apparently so heterodox, ought not, then, to alarm the representatives of the Crocean aesthetic. The grammatical and stylistic elements, insofar as they belong to the economic and juridical world, do not act as an *operating* force in the aesthetic sphere, but only as a *conditioning* activity in the social sphere. Except for this fundamental (and external) difference, stylistics can be defined similarly, in fact in terms almost identical to those

---

[11] Loc. cit., p. 196.

[12] See my *Civiltà del dopoguerra*, Florence, 1956, pp. 105ff.

[13] *Variété*, Paris, s.a. (1924), pp. 89-90, quoted by Fubini, op. cit., p. 7 note.

21

used for literary criticism. For instance, M. Sansone's definition:[14] "That discipline which makes provisional use of all schemes, without attempting to fix of theme, for illustrative or didactic purposes, that discipline which finds the measure of judgment in each text it examines, which is as flexible as the movement and the peculiarities of a literary text, which needs to know the writer's intentions, that is, the expressive reasons and the genesis of the work, and which refuses to arrange the objects of its study into a contiguous series connected by links of necessity or causality, is called neither more nor less than literary criticism."

This definition ought to be corrected in the sense that literary criticism does not need to know the writer's intentions; its object is, rather, to arrive at an understanding of them, interpret them, relive them. But it is very important to note that a simple additional provision renders this definition adequate for stylistics; to be precise, the following: "that discipline which compares all this with the rigidity imposed by the conventions which are valid in the Italian, French or English linguistic community of the time, is called neither more nor less than stylistics."

We arrive at these positive results if our point of departure is the parallelism between juridical and linguistic institutions. Those who, on the other hand, reject this parallelism, those who accept the intrinsic and not only functional identity of thought and expression must also accept the notion that differences between languages, such as those that divide Italian from English, are natural consequences of the spirit in speech. They are, in other words, soon on the way toward such empty notions as the 'spirit' or 'genius' of the Italian or English language (see below), in reality, that is, a *racist* theory, Italian, French, English thought-expression, and so on. The only correct formulations are those of thought (without ethnic attributes) and of expression (whether Italian, English or French).

[14] Loc. cit., p. 205.

22

If the Saussurean *parole* corresponds to criticism, and *langue* to grammar, we need a term which will correspond on the linguistic plane to that third factor which has been called stylistics, and that term is *langue individuelle,* as G. Nencioni and I have defined it,[15] precisely as a notion intermediate between the other two, both well-known and widely accepted.

The accusations of hybridism which have been leveled at it have only an external and apparent validity; they in no way weaken its solidity. Paraphrasing M. Sansone's words,[16] the *langue individuelle* corresponds to a "truer reality of language" just as jurisprudence reflects "a truer reality of the laws."

But there also exists a traditional word corresponding to the notion of the *langue individuelle,* and that word is *style.*

Style is a *relationship* between the creative individual and the society in which he operates. Style is what remains as individual in linguistic creations, as soon as they have entered the economic and juridical world, that is, when they have attained a legality which is external to the individual creator,[17] when, in less technical language, these have become accessible to the reader.

Let no one dare call *stylistics,* when so understood, a "stylistics without style."[18] The nexus between stylistics and style is unmistakable. Only such a stylistics can be, in fact, the science of style correctly anchored to artistic creativity and to the linguistic creations of man. Those who, in defining style, leave out the "reader," that is, the social element, build on sand, no less than those who would define style without allowing for consideration of the author's intentions.

---

[15] Nencioni, *Idealismo e realismo nella scienza del linguaggio,* Florence, 1946. See also my *Studi di stilistica,* pp. 7ff and 15ff.

[16] Loc. cit., pp. 198f.

[17] See Chapter VIII.

[18] Words of H. Jacquier quoted in Schiaffini's foreword to Spitzer, *Critica stilistica e storia del linguaggio,* Bari, 1954, pp. 19-20 note 7.

23

Such is the final parallelism which is established; just as the analysis of the motifs realized in the Saussurean *parole* is performed by criticism, and the analysis of the relationships which govern the structure of the Saussurean *langue* is performed by grammar, so the analysis of the choices of which style is born is performed by stylistics. Stylistics, on this theoretical, pre-juridical plane, has its place in the sun; justified positively by the ceaseless contacts between criticism and grammar, and negatively by the void that separates the aesthetic from the juridical.

II

DEPTH

In the world of critical, stylistic and grammatical experiences, the three areas just described appear at first sight
to be contiguous, on the same plane, and internally homogeneous. Keener scrutiny, however, will reveal a different
picture. Within each area, closer examination of individual
realizations — critical, stylistic and grammatical — makes
clear that a two-dimensional conception of those areas is
inadequate. Recourse must be had to *volume*.

Within the area of criticism, for instance, the foundation of any structure is the act of reading. Not any reading,
of course, but that reading by which, in Spitzer's words,
"we have grasped the meaning of a sentence or a poem —
which then become more than the sum total of their single
words or sounds."[1]

Neither of De Robertis' possibilities, reading in order
to know or knowing in order to read, is applicable; this reading is also knowing.[2] Other more elementary or analytical
modes of reading do not concern us for the moment.

In these circumstances, and only in these, the reader
is automatically a critic. Criticism, then, implies not only[3]
the critic's presence, but also his active participation and
reactions. Such a reader is conscious of his own impressions
and succeeds in expressing them, from the crude statement
'this is beautiful,' 'this is ugly,' to the most refined nuances
and the subtlest distinctions. The first critical manifestations
cannot be represented in terms of the two-dimensional plane

[1] Spitzer, *Linguistics and Literary History*, Princeton, 1948, p. 7.
[2] De Robertis, *Studi*, Florence, 1944, p. 13.
[3] Fubini, *Critica* cit., pp. 36ff.

and the area of it allocated to criticism; they cannot be placed in a specific spot, rather to the right than to the left. Criticism, when so understood, is seen not to spread on such a surface, but to send down roots into the work of art. However elementary such criticism may be, it always suggests the notion of depth with regard to a work of art.

It will then be up to us to establish the image we think preferable — to say with Spitzer[4] that authors 'speak' before they write, or to agree with Fubini[5] that the critic undergoes a catharsis by reëxperiencing the pure word of the artist, or to accept Benda's more comprehensive definition,[6] according to which the critic simply carries on the artist's work and criticism, therefore, is a continuation of the work of art.

More vague, but no less productive, is Foscolo's advice,[7] "The reader while reasoning with the critic, must never cease to feel with the poet." To reason, to feel — the presence of these two terms is sufficient to confirm the existence of a third dimension in even the most elementary criticism, which, even if it appears clearly in the relationship between works of art and criticism, is accentuated within the area of criticism.

Consider the case of Attilio Momigliano, an Italian critic of the so-called impressionist approach. His basic assumptions were not doctrinal but romantic.[8] Outside the well-defined field of aesthetics he tended to enlarge his interests in the direction of the closely related field of psychology, as his classic analyses of the *Divine Comedy* or of *The Betrothed* show.

His spontaneous presence as a reader, dealing with a work of art but still free of any intention to effect an organic reworking of the work, appears in observations like the fol-

[4] Spitzer, *Romanische Stil- und Literaturstudien*, I, Marburg 1931, p. 5.
[5] See his *Critica e poesia* cit., especially pp. 3-9.
[6] Benda, *Atti del convegno del PEN Club*, Venice, 1949; in Fubini, op. cit., p. 4.
[7] Foscolo, as cited in Fubini, op. cit., p. 82.
[8] Fubini, op. cit., p. 421.

lowing: "That is the reason for which there is in *The Little Flowers of Saint Francis* a realism which on rare occasions is even crude — and that astounds us — and always produces in us a clear impression of an atmosphere of poverty . . .[9]; "When we read the satires directed against the aristocracy, the clergy and the classicists, it seems that we can define the poet as a mocker of late arrivals"[10]; "Minetta's voice, hoarse from misery, vice and passion, can never again be forgotten."[11] The spontaneity, the immediacy and the presence of the reader are such that his reactions can be influenced even by the order of his readings: "Alfieri's sonnets must be read after his *Life* and his tragedies,"[12] and "One must not read Leopardi's *Pensieri* after having read Epictetus, Gracián or the great French moralists."[13]

This does not mean that criticism means only consciousness of "impressions" nor does it mean that Momigliano tries to evade the need to rework them. In dealing with Sannazaro's *Arcadia*, he says that, "a patient gatherer of impressions may stop, but not the critic, to whom the continuity and unity of the inspiration are important."[14] His sensitivity in this dimension appears, then, when he distinguishes a "poetry to be dug out and co-ordinated," a "poetry to be conquered," as opposed to poetry that "offers itself immediately to the reader, whole, obvious, and almost plays for him the music he ought to sing."[15] D'Annunzio and Pascoli are put into the first category by Momigliano, and Petrarch, Leopardi, Manzoni and Dante into the second, a distribution which implies, on Momigliano's part, elaboration and judgment rather than spontaneous and unmotivated response. When Momigliano made clear the influence of aesthetic

9 *Studi di poesia*, Bari, 1938, p. 14.
10 ibid., p. 127, concerning Parini.
11 ibid., p. 130, concerning Porta.
12 ibid., p. 112.
13 ibid., p. 140.
14 ibid., p. 53.
15 ibid., p. 239.

27

canons on criticism,[16] he felt the presence of this dimension even though he was not particularly pleased by it. When he denied the possibility of a criticism inspired by the ideas of the hermetic poets and writers,[17] he recognized that there were a clarity and a rationality proper to critical activity which themselves implied an ascent, that is to say a vertical development, a depth in the aesthetic activity of the critic. These rational elements impose themselves energetically when the critic sets more ambitious goals for himself and, beyond his awareness of his impressions, transforms his thoughts from a descriptive and unmotivated into a motivated and an interpretive judgment. And so we have the kind of criticism inspired by Benedetto Croce which is still carried on in Italy by excellent men.[18] From this inspiration derive all-inclusive definitions, such as that of Ariosto as the "poet of harmony",[19] which aim simultaneously at a critical choice and an all-encompassing interpretation.

And yet the vertical dimension is not superfluous even in these definitions. Croce's judgment of Pascoli is not impressionistic; it is, rather, strongly motivated: affectation, superabundance, local patriotism are the objects of his criticism because they distract the reader and lead him away from serious participation in the poetic aspirations of the writer. The first step in the book[20] takes place on another level, however: p. 1, "I am reading some of the most famous of Giovanni Pascoli's poems and they make a strange impression on me. Do I like them? Do I dislike them? Yes, no, I don't know"; p. 3, "The general structure is unpleasantly symmetrical"; p. 6, "The delicate poet has begun to imitate the clucking of the hen again, and the reader finishes with that annoying cry still in his ear." We find ourselves on an impressionistic plane. And then we have, on the other

16 In Fubini, op. cit., p. 389.
17 ibid., p. 442. Cf. also Russo as cited in the same work, p. 93.
18 For example, Russo, *Problemi di metodo critico*, Bari, 1929.
19 Croce, *Ariosto, Shakespeare, Corneille*, Bari, 1920.
20 Croce, *Giovanni Pascoli*, new edition, Bari, 1920.

hand, above and beyond this, one of the most mature and carefully worked-out passages on Ariosto: "The first change which Ariosto's several orders of feelings underwent, as soon as they were touched by the Harmony that sang in the depths of their poet's breast, became apparent in their loss of autonomy, in their submission to a single master, in the shift from the whole to part, from motifs to specific instances, from ends to means, and in the death of them all for the benefit of a new life."[21]

The situation with regard to the stylistic area is in no way different. Analyses of style also present the problem of the vertical dimension; they, too, take place on different levels. In the stylistic area the notion of "reading" acquires an autonomy of its own. At this point "reading" and "knowing" are no longer identical. One of the two mutually exclusive possibilities proposed by De Robertis is realized: "knowing in order to read."

And now let us consider how Manzoni's prose offers the reader (as a judge of style) problems which occur on different levels. Insofar as Manzoni's general attitude toward his story is concerned, what is of interest to the critic is to know that Manzoni appears anxious that his narrative seem objective, an aim for which he prepared himself by studying documents, while he has kept himself as a person out of the story. From the stylistic point of view this is brought out through the sparing but deliberate use of the first-person pronoun, singular and plural, which allows a parallel impersonal introduction of the author in a key passage such as the following[22]:

". . . This conclusion, though arrived at by such plain people, has seemed so true that we have decided to set it down here as the moral of our whole story.

21 I quote from Croce's own selection *Filosofia Poesia Storia*, Naples, 1951, p. 757.

22 *I Promessi Sposi*, ed. Chiari Ghisalberti, Milan, 1954, p. 673; cp. *Fermo e Lucia*, in the same edition, p. 669. The English translation quoted here is by D. J. O'Connor, The Macmillan, Co., New York, 1924, p. 666.

29

For the which, gentle reader, if it has not displeased you entirely, feel thankful to the scribe who wrote it, and a little also to the one who has revised it. But if, on the contrary, we have succeeded only in boring you, be assured that we have not done so on purpose."

These last lines of *The Betrothed* are in fact extraneous to the story which really ends with the preceding paragraph. This corresponds to the particular attitude of Manzoni, who seems to be reading the novel aloud, anxious that his listeners think it a true story, but not too true. Therefore, every so often — and this is particularly obvious toward the end — he separates his own responsibility.

The watchfulness of the man over the narrator poses, therefore, a preliminary stylistic problem of the highest level. Stylistic problems on another level arise however in the same passage; such are, for instance, the choices through which this I, which is so troublesome, is not expressed brutally, by means of the first-person singular pronoun. In the first-person plural of certain verb forms, *abbiam pensato* (we have thought, decided), *fossimo riusciti* (we had succeeded; subjunctive), or in the impersonal verb form *non s'è fatto apposta* (it was not done deliberately), instead of the corresponding singular forms of the first person, *ho pensato, fossi riuscito, ho fatto apposta,* there is clearly an attenuation as opposed to the direct second-person forms with which his listeners are addressed: *vogliatene bene* (feel thankful to; imperative), *credete* (believe, be assured; imperative).

On a 'lower' level some isolated choices may be compared as they differ in the first and last drafts, according to Manzoni's own corrections; *povera gente* (poor people) instead of *donnicciuola* (essentially pejorative diminutive of *donna,* woman), *sugo* (juice) instead of *costrutto morale* (moral construction, theory), *tutta la storia* (the whole story) instead of *tutti gli avvenimenti che abbiamo narrato* (all of the events which we have narrated). All of these are choices uniformly directed toward simplification, toward the spontaneity of the spoken language. In a more circumscribed zone, which does not include the whole of artistic achievement, even stylistics requires a vertical development. The vertical dimension presents itself even where it is no longer a question of reading but rather of analyzing. In grammar the analysis of the structure of a period is one thing, with its more or less proportionate and functional load of independent clauses, while the analysis of the individual syntagmata which follow one another in a clause is something else.

Again, in interpreting the difference between the present perfect (*passato prossimo*) and the preterite (*passato remoto*) of the Italian verb, it is one thing to consider it as a nearer-farther opposition, and quite another to treat it as a difference between a past tied to the present and one which is detached from it, independent of chronology.

Grammar which treats solely of the formal aspect of an imperfect *andavo* (from *andare*, to go) and of its corresponding preterite *andai* is one thing, while it is quite another when it considers the functional side and recognizes that *cadeva in combattimento* (fell in combat; imperfect tense) does not indicate the same syntactic relationship as *arrivava ogni sera alle otto* (arrived every evening at eight o'clock; also imperfect).[23]

It is one thing to talk about the phonetic description of the average pronunciation of the Italian language based on an objective analysis, which distinguishes the Lombard *piace* from the Tuscan *piace*, and quite another to talk about the phonological description, based on the great auditory oppositions of voiced and voiceless consonants (*celo, gelo*), of palatals and gutturals (*cero, caro*).

And finally, a syllabary which is restricted to the pedagogical sphere is one thing and an attempt to describe the linguistic institutions valid in a given area, as, for instance, in Jespersen's *Modern English Grammar*, is another.

[23] Devoto and Massaro, *Grammatica italiana*, third edition, Florence, 1952, p. 150.

No less relevant is the difference of level between the description of a language in the immobility of traditional grammars on the one hand and, on the other, the historicity and dynamism to be found in the so-called synchrony of Ferdinand de Saussure, when it is correctly understood.[24] Only in this last case, that is, only on this last level, does a linguistic system no longer appear to be a raw accumulation of material, even if arranged in an orderly fashion, but rather an organic construction. This construction does not rest on an abstract immobility, but floats dynamically, like a ship, on the ceaseless and, at the same time, orderly motion of those waves which correspond to individual speakers.

These various levels do not admit of parallelism, correspondence or comparisons between one area and another, but remain each enclosed in itself.

If we speak metaphorically of 'higher' and 'lower' it is not to be assumed that impressionistic criticism is, therefore, nearer or more comparable to the stylistics which deals with particular corrections because it stands, geometrically, lower than interpretive stylistics, rather than to the stylistics of the levels of the narrative, nor that it is more comparable to normative grammar than it is to structural and critically synchronic stylistics.

The problems which have led to the use of these metaphors are susceptible of further development in other directions. The attribute 'vertical' and the consequent notion 'depth' remain legitimate and, as a whole, incomplete.

The sole legitimate conclusion is negative; the areas of criticism, stylistics and grammar are not geometrically homogeneous. Each of them shows a fervor, a movement, a dynamism of which it is again necessary to show the many forms in which it can become manifest.

24 See my *Fondamenti della storia linguistica*, pp. 55ff.

III

CIRCLES

Having recognized the turmoil and dynamism within
the three areas of criticism, stylistics and grammar, one
might well wonder, first, whether as much turmoil and dynamism press at the frontiers of the three areas, secondly,
to what extent these frontiers serve to establish distinctions
and, finally, to what extent they may be said to be 'barriers.'
The Introduction to *The Betrothed*, compared to that
to *Fermo e Lucia*, shows, through the elementary and insuperable experience of 'corrections,' the simultaneous presence of critical, stylistic and grammatical problems.

"La Storia si può veramente chiamare una guerra il-
lustre contro la Morte: perchè richiamando dal sepolcro gli
anni già incadaveriti, gli passa di nuovo in rassegna, e li
ordina di nuovo in battaglia."[1]

"L'Historia si può veramente deffinire una guerra il-
lustre contro il Tempo, perchè togliendoli di mano gl'anni
suoi prigionieri, anzi già fatti cadaueri, li richiama in vita,
li passa in rassegna, e li schiera di nuovo in battaglia."[2]

The three stages of the correction are gathered together
here: the aesthetic correction, which substitutes Time for
Death as a central figure and corrects *richiamare dal sepolcro* to read *gli toglie di mano gli anni;* stylistic correction,
which substitutes *già fatti cadaueri* for *incadaveriti* and
schierare for *ordinare in battaglia,* and grammatical or
orthographical correction, where the author writes *li passa*
instead of *gli passa* and *Historia* and *deffinire* in place of
storia and *definire.*

1 *Fermo e Lucia*, ed. cit., III, p. 3.
2 *I Promessi Sposi*, ed. cit., I, p. 3.

One and the same ideal of harmony and moderation of expression is translated into a mode of behavior of classical coherence. The consequences appear in the world of aesthetics as well as in the stylistic and grammatical area. A possibility of communication and co-ordination among these areas, even if not a true continuity among them, is manifest. Like few other writers, Manzoni has effected the organic realization of what Vossler called a *Stilsprache*, a *stylized language* or *stylistic tradition*, as you will.

From a more specific point of view, ceaseless passings back and forth and substantial continuity are found between stylistics and grammar. In the pair *va a casa* and *vai a casa*, which is presented to us as a stylistic choice, the imperative and affective tone of the first element prevails against the cold and matter-of-fact tone of the second.

If I wish a certainty of command such as to admit of no doubt and which will render superfluous the use of a commanding tone of voice, I say *vai a casa* instead of *va a casa*. But I may also wish to avoid the imperative for reasons quite contrary to the notion of courtesy, and use a condescending, good-natured or paternalistic *vai a casa* to the butler or the chauffeur.

The stylistic contradicts the morphological point of view and, at the same time, becomes entangled in it. The possible combinations of the pair *nacque a Firenze nel 1265* and *nasceva in Firenze il 1265* are more numerous and more subtly gradated. The first, and usual, formula implies the occurrence of a momentary action in the past, an abstract reference to the geographical place (Florence) and a precise statement of time, contained in "nel 1265." The second allows three variants which, morphologically, consist in substituting a durative for an instantaneous verb,[3] the substitution of reference in space for the abstract reference *a Firenze*[4] and of reference, for time contained within the year 1265. But at

[3] Devoto and Massaro, *Grammatica italiana*, second reprinting, Florence, 1954, p. 150.
[4] ibid., pp. 238 and 244.

the same time the stylistic point of view underlines, in the three successive forms, a certain emphasis and exceptional quality which does not stand in any necessary relationship to the morphological values. The eight possibilities to which it gives rise reflect eight different combinations derived from normal morphological resources; they are stylistic choices gravitating in three different directions, all of which are, however, less usual. Here, as well, stylistics contrasts the morphological values; it cannot however, do without them.

The continuity between the worlds of grammar and criticism is no less certain, even if less obvious. A paradoxical proof of this is to be found in the fact that we exercise greater mastery of a language the more we are oblivious of the extrinsic norms of its empirical grammar, the more, in other words, we are unconscious of its linguistic conventions. We become aware of them again, we recall them, only when we want to study collective structures rather than interpret texts or listen to those who speak to us.

Certain verses of Giovanni Pascoli fall short not because the inspiration is weak but because onomatopoeia is carried too far in them and thus forces us to abandon a state of divine unconsciousness and reawakens our grammatical sensitivity, overpowering the artistic momentum. Such is the case with the *cocco* of the hen in the poem *Valentino*.[5] Inversely, the aesthetic momentum invades the territory of grammar, making us feel that certain words are 'ugly,' 'pretentious' or 'vulgar.' When Panzini, "taken aback and overcome at the same time" by the neologisms,[6] says that the word *affarista* is "not beautiful" or exclaims, "Oh, what an ugly word!" with regard to the word *affermarsi* in the sense of *to make a name for one's self*, he introduces a negative aesthetic element. In the first case he does so in the context of a fact of exclusively grammatical derivation and in the

[5] Pascoli, *Canti di Castelvecchio*, second ed., Bologna, 1926, pp. 83ff. Cf. Croce's *Giovanni Pascoli*, new edition, Bari, 1920, p. 6.

[6] Schiaffini, "Le nove edizioni di questo dizionario," preface to the *Dizionario moderno* of A. Panzini, ninth edition, Milan, 1950, p. xv.

second of a metaphor in a grammatical framework. It is conceivable that both words may have occurred more than once to Panzini himself and that he may have felt himself interrupted and distracted by a critical motif which had penetrated into the lexical system he controlled as an author, just as we, as readers, are interrupted and distracted by the recollection of the infelicitous onomatopoeias of Pascoli. Thus each of us, within the framework of the common lexicon, has his prejudices and preferences, perhaps unconscious, from the sum of which there is born an individual lexicon or a personal lexical 'style.' We do not know how to explain either the exclusions or the preferences. A good example would be an old teacher of mine in my early youth who would not allow us to use the word *persona* in our compositions. When asked why, he would usually answer that *persona* meant *mask* in Latin.

A judge as free of prejudice as Mario Fubini has recognized[7] that the Crocean definition of criticism finds itself, historically if not theoretically, compressed between two other neighboring forms of criticism, the impressionistic on the one hand and the sociological on the other.

The first does not pose new problems because it has already been assigned to its proper location in which no problems of borders are involved (Chap. II). It forms part of the internal dynamism of aesthetic criticism. The second implies recognition of the fact that interpretive criticism does not find a void on the opposite, impressionistic side.

There is, therefore, a criticism which takes account of the new 'social' fact. That is to say that we pass over onto the very territory in which stylistics operates without having to climb a barrier or to bridge a chasm.

It is not necessary to demonstrate at length the ceaseless flux from the area of criticism in the strict sense of the word, intimately tied to aesthetics and the individual world, toward the area of stylistics, which takes the 'social' element into consideration.

7 Fubini, op. cit., p. 476.

I myself recognized this forcefully when I stated[8] that scholars who study stylistics must take account of the intentions of the authors, that they must, in other words, already have interpreted the authors. Other writers insist on this so much that they identify the stylistic with the aesthetic investigation and, therefore, in fact dissolve the former into the latter; such are G. Contini,[9] M. Fubini,[10] L. Spitzer[11] and M. Sansone.[12]

I will not deny that many of my observations are of a critical nature. They are, however, for that very reason to be considered as 'conditions' for the stylistic work but are not yet stylistic analyses. They prove brilliantly the intimacy of contacts, but they cannot lead to identification, if only because of the fundamental preliminary question pointed out earlier; stylistics begins to assert its sovereignty only when the 'social' notion presents itself, with the consequent relationship of dualism between the author and the community to which he belongs. The continuity is very close, but it is *not* identity.

When one speaks of D'Annunzio's ecstatic musicality,[13] critical appreciation, in a stylistic study, is not an end but a means, to define the musical element as a frame for the D'Annunzian picture in the Italian linguistic community of its time. This latter was the 'end.' When, concerning Proust,[14] I affirm the existence of a break between semantic and syntactic time, I can certainly give a critical definition of the writer's attitude, but the stylistic end is elsewhere, in the placing of that attitude in the picture of the literary language of the time, a language so foreign to the stretching of the sovereignty of the syntactic structures to such a point, that

---

[8] See my *Studi di stilistica*, pp. 32ff.

[9] *Lettere d'oggi*, V (1943), pp. 77-79, and *Lingua nostra*, II (1950), pp. 53ff.

[10] op. cit., p. 121.

[11] Spitzer, *Spettatore italiano*, VIII (1955), pp. 362f.

[12] *Giornale* cit., pp. 204f.

[13] See my *Studi di stilistica*, pp. 130ff.

[14] ibid., pp. 140ff.

it becomes indifferent to the corresponding expressive, or semantic, rhythm. And when[15] I have shown that Italo Svevo's direct discourse is so often nothing more than an adaptation of an indirect structure, a situation in which, consequently, the 'I' of the writer prevails over those which only later have become the actors, I can rejoice that Contini[16] considers this a positive critical result. But for stylistic purposes it is not the artistic personality that counts, it is the problem of the greater or less ease of exchanges between the two planes, which becomes apparent to the reader, a problem, which, for that very reason, has no interest for the pure critic.

In all these cases we shall speak using Karl Vossler's term *Sprachstile*, or 'linguistic styles,' that is, we shall speak of the individual impress which survives in the much debated and sometimes belabored relationship between the individual and his linguistic community.

Stylistics does not simply accept what criticism has worked out. Sometimes it anticipates problems of its own, isolatedly, in the aesthetic sphere, as though the weight of society made itself felt prematurely, or as if an expressive void prematurely opened the way to stylistic points of view.

Consider these three passages from Fogazzaro's *Piccolo Mondo Antico:*

"Discorrevano sempre sottovoce, con una elettricità in corpo che dava luce per gli occhi e scosse per i nervi, assaporando il parlar sommesso con le porte e le finestre chiuse, il pericolo di aver quella lettera, la vita ardente che si sentivano nel sangue, le parole alcooliche a cui tornavano ogni momento."[17]

"Lo zio si alzò e se ne andò per l'uscio del salotto con passo franco, mostrando anche da tergo la sua faccia eretta, il suo modesto ventre pacifico, la sua serenità di filosofo antico. Franco, ritto sul limitare della terrazza, con le braccia

15 ibid., pp. 186f.
16 *Lingua nostra*, II (1950), p. 57.
17 *Piccolo mondo antico*, Part II, chapter II.

incrociate sul petto e le sopracciglia aggrottate, guardava verso Cressogno. Se in quel moment egli avesse avuto fra le mascelle un fascio di Delegati, di Commissari, di birri e di spie, avrebbe tirato tale un colpo di denti da farne una melma sola."[18]

"Aveva sempre pensato, dopo la morte di Maria, che il Libro del Destino nulla potesse più avere di nuovo per lei, che certe intime fibre del suo cuore fossero morte. E adesso una Voce arcana parlava proprio là dentro, diceva: Sappi che nel libro del tuo Destino una pagina si chiude, un'altra si apre. Vi è ancora per te un avvenire di vita intensa; il dramma, che tu credevi finito al secondo atto, continua e deve essere straordinario, se Io to lo annuncio."[19]

Fubini[20] bitterly criticizes these passages, emphasizing the succession of annoying impressions such as the phrases "parole alcooliche" (intoxicating words), "avesse avuto fra le mascelle un fascio di Delegati" (had had a bundle of delegates . . . between his teeth), "avrebbe tirato un tal colpo di denti da farne una melma sola" (would have ground them so hard that all these functionaries would have been reduced to pulp), and so on.

But before we take a position concerning these statements, it will be well to compare the English translation[21]:

"They still conversed in an undertone, with an electric current in their veins, that flashed from their eyes, and made their nerves tingle; enjoying this hushed talk behind closed doors and windows, the danger of being in possession of that letter, the glowing life they felt in their blood, and those intoxicating words they were always repeating."[22]

"Whereupon Uncle Piero rose and went out at the drawing room door with a firm step, and even when his

18 ibid., chapter V.
19 ibid., Part III, chapter II.
20 op. cit., pp. 59ff.
21 English translation by Prichard-Agnetti, London, 1906.
22 ibid., pp. 165f.

back was turned, displaying a head and body erect, and an unruffled serenity like that of an ancient philosopher.

Franco, with knitted brows and arms crossed upon his breast, was standing motionless upon the edge of the terrace, and looking towards Cressogno. If at that moment he had had a bundle of delegates, Commissaries, police-agents and spies between his teeth, he would have ground them so hard that all these functionaries would have been reduced to pulp."[23]

"Since Maria's death she had firmly believed that the Book of destiny could contain nothing new for her, that certain secret fibres of her heart were dead. And now a mysterious voice was speaking within that heart, saying: Know that one page in the book of your destiny is finished, and the leaf has been turned. For you there is still a future of intense living. The drama that you believed had come to an end at the second act, is to continue, and if I myself announce it to you, it must indeed prove wonderful."[24]

A critic whose mother tongue was English could not judge the validity of Fubini's position because of two factors in the translation: Franco's poetic images in his moment of impotent rebellion, Uncle Piero's in his moment of resignation and Luisa's at a turning point in her existence appear with absolute clarity and sense of proportion, in perfect harmony with their respective expressive situations; and the unhappy stylistic choices and the obvious lexical errors of the Italian text are not decisive for the English text and have, therefore, been emended in the translation.

In other words, Fubini's criticism is, in these passages, instinctive and partial. Fubini, unwittingly attracted by the stylistic problem of the lexical choices, does not undertake a true and proper interpretation of the characters, the Uncle, Luisa and Franco, only because they are beclouded by external shadows, peculiar to the Italian linguistic system used by the author, and, for that matter, easily emendable.

[23] ibid., p. 213.
[24] ibid., p. 429.

Of course we could also require of the English translator that he use an equally unhappy choice of words to call
forth, in the English reader, that very revulsion that Fubini
feels when he reads the Italian text. But such zeal would be
excessive, and comparable perhaps to that of the translator
who felt obligated to insert into his translation grammatical
errors and syntactical carelessness similar to those he found
in the original.

Fogazzaro's defects and linguistic *lacunae* are extrinsic
to his expressive reasons. The translation frees Fogazzaro's
creation from incrustations and slag precisely because it remains faithful in those elements which are external to the
expressive substance.

A counterproof can be supplied from D'Annunzio, a
writer, who, as opposed to Fogazzaro, poses difficult problems for translators and who is inevitably denatured by them.
No translator is able to maintain the ornamentality and
musicality that are such an essential part of D'Annunzio's
expressivity. D'Annunzio's stylistic peculiarities are tied to
demands which we may not like, but which are always aesthetic and thus differ from Fogazzaro's unwitting peculiarities. It may be aesthetically advantageous to correct a text
by D'Annunzio, but such correction is always unfaithful,
which is not the case with Fogazzaro.

Consider, for instance, the following passage from the
last 'book' of the *Trionfo della Morte:*

"Ciascuno di quei musici maghi ch'essi prediligevano
tesseva intorno alla loro sensibilità acuita un diverso incante-
simo. Una Pagina di Roberto Schumann evocava il fantasma
d'un amore inveterato che aveva disteso sopra di sé a guisa
d'un artifiziale firmamento il tessuto delle sue memorie più
belle e con una dolcezza attonita e triste lo vedeva a poco
a poco impallidire. Un *Improvviso* di Federico Chopin diceva
come in sogno: 'Odo nella notte quando tu dormi sul mio
cuore, odo nel silenzio della notte una stilla che cade, che
lenta cade, eguale continua cade, così da presso, così
lontano! Odo nella notte la stilla che dal mio cuore cade, lo

stillante sangue che dal mio cuore cade, quando tu dormi, quando tu dormi, io solo.' Alti cortinaggi di porpora, cupi come la passione senza scampo, intorno a un letto profondo come un sepolcro evocava l'*Erotica* di Edoardo Grieg: e una promessa di morte in una voluttà silenziosa; e un ismisurato dominio, ricco di tutti i beni della terra, aspettante invano il suo re scomparso, il suo re nella nuziale e funerale porpora morituro."[25]

"Each one of the musical wizards whom they loved cast over their acutely sensitive imaginations a fresh spell. A *Blatt* of Robert Schumann evoked the vision of a love long dead, who in lieu of a firmament had stretched above him a tissue woven of his fairest memories, and now, with sad and gentle amazement, saw them fade and pale by slow degrees. An *impromptu* of Chopin murmured as in a dream 'I hear in the night when thou slumberest on my heart, in the silence of the night, I hear a drop that falls, that slowly falls, that ever falls — now near, now far. I hear in the night the drop that falls from my heart, the blood that drop by drop falls from my heart when thou slumberest — thou slumberest and I am alone.' Sumptuous curtains, crimson and sombre as a relentless passion, surrounding a bed deep as a tomb — such was the picture, called up by the *Erotique* of Edvard Grieg, and more than that — a promise of death in the silence of rapturous desire; a kingdom, rich without end in all the goods of the earth, waiting in vain for its vanished King, its King expiring amid the nuptial and funeral crimson."[26]

A number of things which are external pedantry have been eliminated, while a genuine archaism, the second-person singular of the verb, shows responsibility and artistic sensitivity. The substantial, cadenced, almost obsessive harmony is respected, as is necessary. An error like *inveterato* translated as *long-dead,* an inadequacy such as *morituro* rendered

---

[25] Edizione dell'Oleandro, Rome, 1934, p. 521.

[26] English translation by Georgina Harding, London, 1898, p. 277.

as *expiring*, do not detract from this difficult critical as well as stylistic feat. And still the translator's personality imposes itself on the English, at once improving and misrepresenting the original.

The answer, therefore, to the original question is negative. The frontiers of criticism, stylistics and grammar are not *barriers*. Thus we justify the image of the circle as it appears after the image of area and that of depth.

Naturally the circle does not necessarily suppress the preceding images, nor is it appropriate to examine the conditions necessary for its successful adaptation, to think up, in other words, the figure of a cylinder with its external surface, its circular sections and its height.

And yet, as in the case of the "areas," neither are two dimensions sufficient for the circle. Without wishing to have recourse to the image of Dante's circles in Hell, the circle, thus understood, is in reality a skein of circular itineraries which occur at different heights, which allow entanglements or intermediate bonds between one and another. In fact, when it passes from the sector of the theoretical spirit to that of the practical spirit the circular itinerary is sundered and gives rise to circles disposed on several planes. Inversely, more than one itinerary converge on the stylistic plane, from the world of the theoretical spirit.

We cannot speak of a circle, but of *circles*, or, still more accurately, of circular itineraries. Let us take the example of Dante's *Paradise*, considered in different lights by Benedetto Croce[27] and Michele Barbi.[28] The former moves on a rigorously aesthetic plane and eliminates from the last canto a whole series of *terzine* of a didascalic and theological nature. Even though they are in harmony with the medieval doctrine of art, these latter are of no interest to aesthetics; they are not poetry. The latter, Barbi, who moves on a primarily historical and cultural plane, recognizes the dif-

---

27 Croce, *Filosofia poesia storia*, pp. 732ff.

28 Barbi in the *Enciclopedia italiana*, vol. XII, p. 340.

ference between our artistic vision and the medieval vision and, therefore, between Dante's creation and our sensitivity; he insists, however, on the motifs of unity rather than on those of selection.

Stylistic examination does not even utilize everything that survives Croce's severe choice. The image of Sleep as it appears in the three *terzine* that begin *Qual è colui che somniando vede*[29] survives not only in its linguistic aspects, but also in its literary and cultural aspects. But stylistic examination avails itself, with absolutely equal right, of all the other *terzine*, those that fall under a negative aesthetic judgment, because, even though they come from a logical and technical plane, it is equally necessary to place them in the linguistic community, according to the same schemes and conventions of which Dante availed himself in his truest poetry.

The circular itinerary does continue, undifferentiated, uninterrupted, but the planes on which it occurs are no longer the same; aesthetics, logic and technique converge and together they distribute themselves in new forms which we call stylistics, literature and cultural *milieux*.

For the same reasons even a telegram, or a bureaucrat's dough draft, in quite the same way as the didactic or oratorical parts of the *Divine Comedy*, are of interest to stylistics, and have a style.

The image of the circle in connection with spiritual experiences is not new. But, before we state its other characteristics in precise terms, it is necessary to discard those images which are recalled by that of the circle in a unilateral or arbitrary way and which are, in reality, only movements which come back to their point of departure. Such is Fubini's case[30] when he speaks of a movement of the center of the expression to the specific details of the periphery and vice-versa. Such also is Spitzer's case[31] when he speaks of

29 Croce, *Filosofia poesia storia*, p. 737.
30 Fubini, op. cit., pp. 110.
31 Spitzer, *Linguistics and Literary History*, pp. 19-20.

44

a "Zirkel im Verstehen," attributed by Dilthey to Schleiermacher, and recognizes a ceaseless, now inductive and now deductive motion in his own work.

This second image can become acceptable only if it undergoes the fundamental correction proposed by Alfredo Schiaffini, who says[32] that, "rather than of an inductive procedure we ought to speak . . . of intuition and divination." That is to say, while in Spitzer's formulation the inductive-deductive alternative is maintained on the level of applied logic, in Schiaffini's the constant succession of aesthetic intuition and logical deduction gives a concrete image which, with good reason, approaches that of the circle.

Whoever, furthermore, examines the essays collected by Spitzer for this purpose[33] realizes that he applies, in fact, a circle more than once, without saying so exactly, without, that is, being completely aware of it.

Only the circularity of the experiences defined by Croce corresponds to the ideal image of a circle. And in it there inheres the uninterrupted continuity, which we have just delineated, from the sector of criticism to that of stylistics and to that of grammar whence, again, back to the sector of criticism. It is a ceaseless passing from the world of the individual to the world of the social in all its gradations, which finally ends up back in that of the individual.

The positivistic objection that this is a vicious circle does not hold.[34] The fallacy of the vicious circle is valid in natural history (Chapter X) when one datum is based on another, and not vice-versa. Here it is a question of taking notice of experiences which suceed one another; the arbitrary choice of one of them as a beginning is not a right or an abuse, but a duty and a necessity.

---

[32] In his foreword to Spitzer's *Critica stilistica* cit., p. 11.

[33] In *Linguistics and Literary History* cit.

[34] Bloomfield, *Language*, XX (1944), pp. 45ff., especially pp. 53ff. Cf. Spitzer, ibid., pp. 245-251.

Concerning this circularity we repeat what Croce said on the subject of the fate of the old philosophical categories:

"They have made room for the eternal circle of the eternal values or forms or categories of the spirit, each one of which, in its operation, presupposes the others, all of which are necessary, and none of which has primacy, because primacy belongs only to the circle, that is to say, only to the spirit itself as a whole."[35]

"Since the forms of the spirit are all necessary, they are all necessarily of like dignity and tolerate only an order of succession and implication which is not hierarchical, for, because of the circularity or circulation of the spiritual life, none of them yields the absolute beginning and none the absolute end."[36]

"These artificial and sometimes monstrous constructions collapse and are swept away as soon as we pass from the symbol of the 'peak' to that of the 'circle.' . . . Poetry is poetry in that it is neither a logical formation nor a practical action; neither is it more purely poetry the more it is free of this or that attitude, and, being what it is and operating as it does, it is antecedent to the logical character of thought as this logical character is antecedent to the practical character of action; nor is it possible to place it elsewhere."[37]

It suffices to substitute stylistic for logical judgment and grammatical for practical judgment to have an exact Crocean formulation and an intrinsically mature definition of this circularity.

---

[35] Croce, *Filosofia poesia storia*, pp. 9f.

[36] ibid., p. 51.

[37] ibid., pp. 75f.

IV

SPACE-TIME

Not even the image of the circles is exhaustive. The irrepressible dynamism that reigns in them, the continual breaking and reëstablishing of the seams give rise to the question whether outside classical geometry we ought not to have recourse to Einsteinian geometry with its fourth dimension, Time.

If we introduce the notion of movement into the images so far described, we must be certain that this notion has the essential characteristic of time, the characteristic of being 'one-way.' What has been said so far ought to be susceptible of more precise statement which would include the determination of time; critical interpretation is not the condition but rather the preëxisting datum of stylistics; the social characterization of the texts, in other words stylistics, is not the condition but the preëxisting datum of grammar; grammatical consciousness is not the condition but the preëxisting datum of criticism, which is, in turn, the preëxisting datum for the study of stylistic relationships. The circle is not closed, as is the image on paper, but, rather, ceaselessly generated like that of a merry-go-round in motion in Luna Park. We can climb onto the merry-go-round at any given moment without looking to see whether the horse or seat that falls to us by chance is in the critical, stylistic or grammatical sector, and with no effect, derived from this indifference, on the motion and functional character of the circle. The direction of movement, however, always remains the same.

The Linguistic Preëxisting Datum. It has been said, in connexion with the continuity of grammar and criticism, that grammatical situations survive in criticism and that critical situations make themselves felt in our grammatical preferences.

It is not a question of a double motion. In the first case the natural light that emanates from our linguistic knowledge fixes on the work of art which is the object of our reading. We profit from it as much as necessary for that interpretation. The result is total. Nothing remains outside the beam of light which misses nothing and is, in great part, superfluous.

The critical illuminations that have repercussions on grammar are reflected lights. As many times as we have read about *affaristi* or *affermazioni sportive*, we have preserved a particular memory of them, perhaps unpleasant, as in Panzini's case, but which throws a very special shadow, without, however, affecting the lexical system as a whole (See above, p. 35). Even if we take an immense text, the *Divine Comedy*, for example, it is only a unilateral and partial preëxisting datum for acquiring a knowledge of the Italian language, but, on the other hand, a knowledge of the body of Italian linguistic institutions is a preëxisting datum for reading the *Divine Comedy*.

Certainly it is on the basis of the texts that the systematic grammar of a language is worked out, but this happens through a complex template superimposed on the texts which are interpreted. This template is not to be identified with the segment of the circle which joins grammar to criticism, which will be the object of a detailed examination later in these pages.[1]

Some of Leo Spitzer's formulations refer to the critical preëxisting datum. The first, strangely reticent and not very logical, consists in not offering resistance to the idea that critical judgment precedes stylistic judgment.[2] But the responsibility, in accepting or rejecting this succession, is in-

---

[1] See Chapter X.

[2] Spitzer, *Spettatore italiano*, VIII (1955), pp. 358ff.

divisible. It cannot be reduced to a dismissal for lack of evidence, for that is not an acquittal. Spitzer is amazed, then, as though by a paradox, by the fact that an achieved and accepted interpretation is a matter close to the heart of the student of stylistics, and, on the contrary (See above) that a knowledge of the languages must precede the critical interpretation. If he "is not opposed" to the priorities of criticism, he must accept this unavoidable consequence.

More serious, on the other hand, is the objection which I have in fact justified through some too drastic formulations of the 'finality' of critical interpretations.

It is a fact that critical judgments are never either collective or final. Their acceptance does bring about a situation in which the stylistic judgment, valid only if it refers to a preceding critical interpretation, is not truly objective — or final, either. But this produces no inconvenience. Since we are dealing with spiritual experiences, represented symbolically in Space-Time, any description of experiences is a chapter in the history of the spirit, of an individual spirit which never finds itself twice in the same circumstances and is, therefore, always different. The preëxisting datum is not for that reason any less valid. An anonymous reader of Spitzer has recognized, and very acutely, that even Spitzer himself does not escape from this demand; he always proceeds, sometimes unwillingly, by taking generalities as his point of departure, the meaning of the whole work of art, right from the beginning.[3]

In this way we confirm that the limit separating criticism from stylistics is not mechanical. In my stylistic studies, the critical preëxisting datum is always present, even though always in different measure. In the case of D'Annunzio[4] the critical preëxisting datum has a greater importance and the strictly stylistic aspect comes to occupy, relatively speaking, a spot of secondary importance; it is, therefore, a merito-

3 Spitzer, *Linguistics* cit., p. 26.
4 See my *Studi di stilistica*, p. 129.

rious labor from the point of view of criticism, and is not by any means accomplished from the stylistic viewpoint.

In the case of Pascoli[5] the stylistic equilibrium is more respected and, probably, the critical preëxisting datum is weaker. The construction is, in this case, objectively balanced, but the foundations have been less exhaustively studied.

It is not, therefore, a question of my having brought to bear two different stylistics. I have, simply, written stylistic works with different centers of gravity. The principle which informs my stylistics remains one.

Still, if we had to proceed on the basis of the different importance of the introductory critical part, and of its greater or less intrinsic validity, it would be possible to speak not only of *two* stylistics of mine, but of the many stlistics made use of by me at one time or another, in proportions which are always different with respect to criticism as such.

After Spitzer, various statements by Mario Fubini deserve attention. Inasmuch as he regarded with suspicion analyses of literary works by linguists and, therefore, linguistics itself, he says (very well)[6] that linguistic criticism "must, all the while treating as understood the conclusions at which another criticism has arrived, emphasize, in its coherence, the linguistic system peculiar to the particular writer." I am, however, less zealous than Fubini in the sense that a writer may have an individual language which is not compact and coherent, which cannot be fitted into a unique and organic system.

In other cases, Fubini's statements, if not accepted, may be merely rectified. The historic vision of the activities of critics and linguists resolves all of the problems provided that it is applied in an organic way. We cannot speak, for instance, of critics and linguists helping "each other,"[7] thus

5 ibid., pp. 193ff.
6 Fubini, op. cit., p. 19.
7 ibid., p. 48.

simply juxtaposing them; the work of the latter begins only when the task of the former has been completed. We may accept the inclusion of aesthetic criticism in a general historical, social and political vision, and also the polemic against poetry separated from literature[8] provided it is clear that these moments introduce the collective factor and are, therefore, later with regard to aesthetic criticism. We may accept Fubini's thesis according to which the description of the style and the definition of the inspiring feeling are only a *momentum* of the judgment,[9] provided that it is recognized that the judgment is quite distinct in its two phases, individual criticism and collective stylistics. In this historical vision the debate between the unitary thesis of Vossler,[10] which holds that the stylistic and aesthetic aspects are inseparable, and Spitzer's non-unitary thesis,[11] according to whic ha distinction is justified, is otiose.

Both theses are legitimate and can be fitted into this higher historicity, through which there is continuity and, at the same time, succession, that is, distinction.

Precisely because he has never participated in the preoccupation of his critical activity outside of aesthetics, Attilio Momigliano has always been cold in the face of the literary fact[12] that is detached from individual sensitivity and, then, enters the sum total of the facts of culture, which are, therefore, several. But insofar as style is concerned he does retreat and his most felicitous statements always respect the priority of the inspiration.

Such, for instance, are his energetic statements concerning Sarpi: "Perhaps not only his studies in the exact sciences and in philosophy, but also that dominant but real leaning of his toward Protestantism, that spirit of his, guilt-

8 ibid., pp. 32ff., and 75.
9 ibid., p. 111.
10 Vossler, *Deutsche Literaturzeitung*, XLV (1924), pp. 1963ff.
11 Spitzer, *Stilstudien*, II, Munich, 1928, p. 523 note 1.
12 *Studi di poesia*, Bari, 1938, pp. 88 and 92.

less of all mundanity, may explain the appearance of his prose, the driest and most circumspect in our whole literature." And in the conclusion, after having pointed out the salient passages, he concludes: "You are often overcome by this restless style in which the mechanism is continuously modelling itself on a concentric motivation . . . The syntax and the vocabulary are of an almost violent Latinity . . ."[13]

The following, on the contrary, is, concerning Fogazzaro, the attentive examination of the salient characteristics of his *Daniele Cortis,* from which he derives — and it is easy to understand why — only *one* single observation on the style· "Certainly those *mots* and those verses are well chosen, to indicate Elena's ardent, pure and sad spirituality, and they, like the titles — "Per lui, per lui!," "Voci nel buio," "Eran degni di questo," "Come gli astri e le palme" — constitute one of the significant peculiarities of Fogazzaro's style."[14] An author who was so typically asocial from the linguistic point of view could only hold Momigliano back from taking other positions concerning style.

And here is a gem, in this succession from aesthetic interpretation to stylistic judgment, concerning the *Fioretti di San Francesco* (*The Little Flowers of Saint Francis*):

"You cannot separate the sacrifices of the little brothers from their miserable places, from the huts, from the village greens crowded with peasants and mischievous youngsters who pull their hoods, push and shove them, and cover them with dirt, just as you cannot separate them from the solitary and mute forests and from that landscape which, through the power of St. Francis, seems even now the most contemplative in the world. You never again forget the winter countryside, where the Saint shows to brother Lion 'those things which are perfect joy' because that is a unique scene in the book. But from all the visions and meditations of the *Little Flowers* there breathes continually a suggestion

---

13 *Studi di poesia,* Bari, 1938, pp. 88 and 92.

14 ibid., p. 211.

of holy solitude, because of a more religious than descriptive power. The words, accented on the penult, and the placid and equal rhythm depict, without seeming to do so, a limpid landscape within which the soul naturally becomes clearer and sees the hidden and vital truths. The prose of the *Little Flowers* is precisely a prose of rapture, of gentleness and affection."[15] Any reader is able easily to confirm the truth of this statement by inspecting the sentence-structure and vocabulary.

Thus literary creation passes from the aesthetic world to social and stylistic consecration. Language-poetry adapts to the schemes of language-instrument, or combats it. The attribution of an 'ideal priority' to speech-poetry over speech-instrument[16] is transformed into — or, if you prefer, is integrated with — the notion of 'chronological priority.'

And here is the counterproof. Stylistic analysis produces brilliant light — but only reflected light; it is incapable of an all-inclusive illumination. Such, for instance, is the following example, taken from the very accurate analyses by De Robertis of a fragment of Foscolo's *Grazie:* "In order less to disturb the reader . . .; of this Silvano he will say only that he is a Silvano . . . He will make him play the 'avena,' but he will not describe the sound; he will say that his house is a shelter of branches and leaves . . . he will intone certain words: *io* (I) . . ., *odo* (hear), *ei* (he), *suon* (sound), *chiama* (calls): and among the pauses, a silence about him cadenced precisely by that pause, distant Florence, lost to the gaze (vague) and the winds remain silent . . . (Silvano hears) even the hermits, still. Olden times have returned, stopped, the present, remote, has disappeared."[17]

It could not be said better. But these examples are one thing if we imagine them preceded by *because* and something else if by *indeed*. Insofar as interpretation of the pas-

15 ibid., pp. 14f.
16 Fubini, op. cit., p. 351.
17 *Studi*, Florence, 1944, pp. 133ff.

sage by the reader is concerned, here, in fact, it is only a question of *indeed*, that is, of stylistic or even lexical exemplification of what De Robertis has already understood. Still, De Robertis has here set himself aims other than merely the interpretation of a circumscribed passage: a rereading "aimed at an essentially artistic end, to clarify, in other words, the birth, the progress and the value of all of the poetry" of an author.[18] When, still dealing with the *Grazie*, he compares the *Suon d'avena*, of the last version, with an earlier variant, *arguto suon d'avena*, he holds that the author has concentrated on accompanying the figure of this Silvano, flying over the sound; and when the hermits become *taciti* for the earlier *pallidi*, an extrinsic detail disappears and the passage harmonizes better with the silence that is the dominant motif of the fragment. In these two cases the *because* is justified, but a passing from the stylistic to the critical level does not follow from this. De Robertis is no longer the critic without attribute here, a pure historian of spiritual experiences which he makes understandable and accessible to others, he is here the *reconstructor* of a text and of the figure of an artist and, therefore, finds himself on other ground, which will be illustrated in Chapter X.

To the question posed by Terracini,[19] whether stylistics is of use to aesthetics or history, there can be no doubt concerning the answer: it is of use to *history*.

The Stylistic Preëxisting Datum. The historical and etymological dictionaries indicate the date of the first known occurrence of a word; an example, chosen from among geometrical terms in French, is *cathète*, attested from 1547 on. The Italian term *cateto* is its descendant. Those same dictionaries then indicate the tie, now broken, between the word and its etymon, for example the same word derived from the mediaeval Latin *cathetus* which in turn is derived from

18 ibid., p. 114.

19 *Archivio glottologico italiano*, XXXV (1950), p. 110.

the Greek *kathetos* which means *let, put down.*[20] They do not, on the other hand, indicate the process by which the word has attained individuality and autonomy.

The nearer origins of a word are constantly stylistic; that is to say that individuality and autonomy, in each case, are attained after a shorter or longer period, during which it represented not an absolute value but rather an alternative. An example is *veclus* in competition with *senex* before it triumphed in the exclusive form *vecchio* (See above, Chapter I).

But, in addition to the nearer origins, there are also remote origins, and these latter consist of an aesthetic creation, which is not necessarily poetic, which corresponds to its first manifestation by an individual. One individual first associated the image of 'prisoner of the Devil' with the word *captivus.* A 'chorus' followed his lead, for whom *cattivo* was 'the Prisoner *par excellence.*'[21] An even larger chorus then carried *cattivo* into the semantic niche of *malo.* Thus, first there was someone who defined the torrential rains of the South as the splashing of water (**plowet;* Lat. *pluit;* cf. Gr. *pleî,* 'navigates') as opposed to the calm rains of the North.

Other pioneers have instead invented words with a motivation which was linguistic as well as aesthetic, or with an exclusively linguistic motivation. An example of the former is *portabagagli* which takes the place of *facchino* by an aesthetic impulse and a linguistic technique; an example of the latter is supplied by the FIAT official who first defined the FIAT "500" by purely linguistic means, as opposed to the other, exclusively aesthetic neologism *topolino.*

Appearances to the contrary notwithstanding, all of these creations are homogeneous, they are all properly in the field of aesthetics even if occasionally we must speak

[20] Battisti and Alessio, *Dizionario etimologico italiano,* I, Florence, 1950, p. 813.

[21] ibid., pp. 817ff.

of a 'zero' aesthetic value. They are a-poetic, not anti-poetic creations, lacking in poetry but not belonging to a field of spiritual activity which excludes poetry. We are surely in the field of individual creations, whatever the mechanism may be that has governed them. We will be faced, in reading the *Paradiso*, with a theological *terzina* rather than a poetical *terzina*, with one of Churchill's telegrams instead of a love letter. But we are always confronted by an individual creation which was first offered as a choice to the lexical treasury of the community and which has since acquired an absolute value and has become grammaticalized.

To paraphrase Spitzer's formula,[22] not only *nihil est in syntaxi quod prius non fuerit in stylo*, but also *nihil est in grammatica quod prius non fuerit in stylo* (that is, the etymon, the key, the preëxisting datum of grammar is always a fact of style); *nihil est in oratione quod prius non fuerit in grammatica* (that is, the etymon, the keyì the preëxisting datum of the discourse consists of the linguistic system); *nihil est in stylo quod prius non fuerit in oratione* (that is, the etymon, the key, the preëxisting datum of the facts of style is in the expressive substance of the discource).

The stylistic preëxisting datum is indispensable. Every creation, whether poetic or a-poetic, is passed from the individual realm through the stylistic sieve of the community, and may continue along the road leading to admission into the linguistic system and become the open patrimony of all citizens; it may also fall back, splendid and ephemeral, immersed and buried in the texts in which it was offered and sterilely proffered as, for example, is the case of Dante's *sene* in the *Paradiso* (XXXI, 59 and 94).

There is also the case of the periphrastic designations of hunger in Spitzer's famous books: "ce l'ò indosso io la *morosa*" (p. 22); "la *signora* aumenta" (p. 40); "la *strega*" (p. 41); "la *negra*" (p. 42); "che *spazzola* abbiamo"

22 Spitzer, *Die Umschreibungen des Begriffes Hunger im Italienischen*, in the series *Beihefte zur Zeitschrift für romanische Philologie*, No. 68 (1920).

(p. 53); "ho gran *lupa*" (p. 54); "soffro molto di *rug-gine*" (ai denti) (p. 63); "la *batissa*" (badessa) (p. 108).

The semantic creativity of which these examples are such obvious proof still belongs only to the fields of aesthetic criticism; these periphrases for hunger, not recognized as true stylistic choices, have remained closed up in the outmoded world in which they were born, one-word poems, not new acquisitions of the Italian lexicon.

But it is a one-way road. There are express trains which, simply because they do not stop at intermediate points, need not use a different track. There are local trains that run only between two points without in any way annulling the reality of other sections of the same line. What is essential is not to talk of true innovations until we begin to move not only in the critical but also in the stylistic field.[23] Every stylistic fact escapes the creativity of the individual. It cannot restore its strength by "returning" to the realm of the individual (as opposed to the collective). Either it becomes grammaticalized or it dies.

Time, with its sense of obligation, is indeed inseparable from this circle; it is congeneric to it. It is a question of the individual or of the social world. And here is the counterproof.

In the example first cited, *vetulus* vs. *senex,* we have been present at the withdrawal of *senex* from the grammatical world of the lexicon to the stylistic world where it is an alternative choice with an archaic flavor for the rising *vetulus* (Chapter I).

But this passage from the one to the other does not invalidate the theory. It indicates the impoverished vitality, the involutive motion, the beginning of *senex'* journey toward death.

To speak more generally, any search for distant connections, against the current of history, leads us to recognize distinctions and instructive but now dead ties. In Emerson's

---

[23] Terracini, in *Archivio glottologico italiano*, XXXVIII (1953), p. 29,

essay *The Poet*[24] the antithesis between poetic and lexified words is exceedingly well described:

"The poet made all the words, and therefore language is the archives of history, and . . . a sort of tomb of the muses . . . Language is fossil poetry."

These words of Emerson, to which it is quite proper to subscribe at a distance of 118 years, are very far from Spitzer's concerning etymology.

According to Emerson, etymology "finds the deadest word to have been once a brilliant picture;" while according to Spitzer,[25] "an etymology introduces meaning into the meaningless."

Less poetically than Emerson we shall say that etymology restores a retrospective dependence to words which, having come to age and having been listed in the dictionaries, had freed themselves from it and had forgotten it. Floating along with the current of time, we choose between what survives and what dies, but nothing is allowed to be lost. Going against the current we reconstruct specific facts, but we do not fill in empty spaces.

Critical-grammatical experience, with its interpretations, does not consist, therefore, as Spitzer says,[26] of the "universal search for an etymon." On the contrary, it consists of the exact definition of the place occupied by words and constructions in a stylistic milieu, whatever their origin may have been, poetic or a-poetic, intuited or accepted, unsought and undiscussed.

Of course, the search for etyma, etymology, and comparative grammar exist, but they go against the current of history and belong to a completely different area of activity. (Chapter X). In the realm of space-time which we are considering, there is only one passage, from the aesthetic (posi-

---

24 Emerson, Ralph Waldo, *The Poet*, in *Essays*, second series (1844), cited from the edition published in Philadelphia, 1896, p. 22. Cf. Fubini, op. cit., p. 348.

25 Spitzer, *Linguistics* cit., p. 6.

26 Schiaffini in Spitzer's *Critica stilistica* cit., p. 10.

tive or indifferent) creation to juridical recognition, from liberty to discipline.

For this reason we recognize the basic aestheticity of all linguistic creations and, at the same time, its irrelevance to the end of defining the nature of linguistic systems.[27] In just this way the raising of negroes to a status of equality and the racial desegregation currently in progress are born of exigencies or sensitivities of a moral order. No one would dare define the laws imposed by the one and the other as moral rather than juridical laws.

And still the juridical laws have a constructive influence, not only in that they forbid some things but also on the activities of men. In the same way grammatical knowledge makes itself felt on men's capacity to understand and interpret a text.

From the shadows of this historicity, classification, the soul of the traditional procedures of the natural sciences, appears again as a means and not as an end. As Fubini has said, it "is not the end of historical judgment."[28] And as John Dewey has said, "The fallacy of definition is the other side of the fallacy of rigid classification, and of abstraction when it is made an end in itself instead of being used as an instrument for the sake of experience . . . For practical purposes we *think* in terms of classes, as we concretely experience in terms of individuals."[29]

By recognizing, in accord with Crocean methodology, that classifications are instruments of command and are heuristic formulas, we affirm the perennial variety and unclassificability of the real. A Crocean scholar like M. Sansone[30] mistakenly protests against the common statement "that reality is richer than any doctrine." In the face of

[27] Spitzer, *Stilstudien* II, pp. 514-520.

[28] Fubini, op. cit., p. 148.

[29] Dewey, *Art as Experience*, New York, 1934, p. 216f. Cf Fubini, op. cit., p. 256.

[30] *Giornale* cit., p. 197.

reality any formula is by definition arbitrary and does violence to it. Orthodoxy — whether idealistic or positivistic is not important — cannot by its very nature prevail against it.

The uninterrupted continuity of all these experiences through the individuality of the theoretical realm and the sociality of the practical realm reappears, luminous, above all the classifications which have been attempted upon it.

The homogeneity and continuity of the circle is given, then, by the permanent subjectivity of experiences, even when these refer to the world of the practical spirit.

When that equivalent of a magistrate, the scholar, devoted to stylistic questions, draws up his sentences, defining a relationship between the judicial act of the individual and the conventions recognized by the community, he leaves an indelible personal imprint on that definition.

If in a dictionary the definitions of individual words do not follow automatically from the sum of the examples gathered, but are born alive of the sensitivity of the lexicographer, an authorized representative of the linguistic community, that must mean that this subjective imprint is affirmed also in the study of the lexicon.

Even in the more jealous and stable field of morphology this individual interpretation of the linguistic system takes precedence over the objective interpretation. In Italian there are pairs of words like *volta, svolta; fatto, sfatto*. The distinctive sign is furnished by the initial alternation of *s-* and zero. What does it mean? The temptation of the grammarian — even of a high level — is to give one and only one meaning to all the *s-*'s. And this Brøndall[31] has tried to do. But the average Italian speaker does not submit to this unity; he feels that the relationship between *fatto* and *sfatto* is one of negation or opposition, while that between *volta* and *svolta* is one of reinforcement. He associates *sfatto* and *scarico* on the one hand, and *svoltare* and *scaldare* on the

---

[31] *Acta Linguistica*, II (1940-41), pp. 151-164.

other. And he distinguishes the two groups in spite of the common initial consonant. That is to say that the linguistic system carries within itself incrustations justified by history but no longer functional; such is the reflected light thrown on these formations by their respective 'superlatives,' which are *dis-* for the first group (*disfatto, discarico*), and *ris-* for the second (*risvolta, riscaldare*). If the investigation is carried further it is observed that a classification into two categories, approximately correct for the average ear, does not suffice for a more sensitive ear. In the *Mélanges Bally*[32] I have justified four groups, distinguishing, in addition to provenience and negation, the intensity of *smunto* and *sperduto* and the durative character of *sdoppiare* and *scorrere*, in comparison to the weaker *munto* and *perduto* and to the momentary *doppiare* and *correre*. In this interpretation of the Italian linguistic system I have used my individual sensitivity no differently from the critic who has analyzed a verse by Pascoli and has found in it fine distinctions which another critic denies. This happens because in every historical exposition (and the description of a linguistic system has its own historicity),[33] the intrinsic, fundamental element is artistic and not rational or scientific, as Benedetto Croce had shown as early as 1893,[34] whether it is a question of ethical-political, linguistic, economic or juridical history.

The whole method, therefore, consists not of applying external schemes or "pegs" (in von Wartburg's terminology) or *Erlebnisse,* according to the definition of the method which, in relation only to criticism, Friedrich Gundolf[35] had given: "die Aufgabe des Bildungshistorikers ist der des Übersetzers verwandt, nicht der des Grammatikers."

[32] *Mélanges Bally,* Geneva, 1939, pp. 263-269.

[33] See my *Fondamenti di storia linguistica,* pp. 55ff.

[34] Croce, "La storia ridotta sotto il concetto generale dell'arte," in *Primi saggi,* second edition, Bari, 1927, chap. I.

[35] Gundolf, *Goethe,* twelfth edition, Berlin, 1925, pp. 6f. Cf. Spitzer, *Linguistics* cit., p. 1.

V

INTERSECTING PLANES

If we now consider in the space-time (chronotopos) thus defined the concrete realizations, the individual works of art, we find, whatever the linguistic system chosen in any given case — English, Italian, French — that they appear as intersecting planes.

This multiplicity must be justified in the face of an objection of a theoretical nature, energetically formulated by Dewey, among others,[1] the 'indivisibility of art.'

The problem, non-existent or refuted from the point of view of criticism, presents itself from the stylistic point of view in such a way that it must be dealt with, not as a question of literary *genres*, which constitute schemes of a naturalistic character (Chapter X), but as a question of the relationship between *narrator* and *narratum*, as they inevitably take shape — and in an infinitely varied way — once the artistic expression has been realized through the linguistic institutions.

The fundamental nucleus of the point of departure can be found in the notions of the lyric, the grammatical and the epic, notions which are classificatory but quite legitimate in criticism.

The formal equivalences of these dominant expressive *momenta* can be summed up in the following way: the tripartite division which the linguistic institutions offer the artist consists of the possibility of making his realizations gravitate in the sphere of the 'I', of the 'You' or of the 'He', in accord with a characteristic fundamental to the structure of

[1] Cp. Dewey, *Art as Experience*, chap. IX, The Common Substance of the Arts (New York, 1934, p. 187-213).

the languages of our cultural world, which is Indoeuropean-classical-Christian.

The informing principle and the application are different in that, according to the literary *genres*, there is a rigid tripartite division with the consequent responsibilities which are incumbent upon the author, and with the eye fixed on the greater or less adhesion to the canons which are fixed in advance for each *genre*. According to the stylistic point of reference the tripartite division is external to the author, and the interest in the investigation is not in the coherent prevailing of the one or of the other, but, on the contrary, in the degree in which both, and others as well, present themselves, contrast and merge.

If this analysis is now external to the author, it is not true that we are thereby relieved of the obligation to carry out a preliminary interpretation of the author, with the appropriate analyses of the lyric-dramatic and epic *momenta*, which succeed each other in the work of art. What is important is that the stylistic sphere of the 'I' does not, in fact, become identified with the aesthetic notion of the lyric, nor the sphere of the 'You' with the notion of the dramatic, nor the sphere of the 'He' with the notion of the epic.

The first determination which imposes itself in this case is quantitative in nature. On the one hand we may have a presentation which harmonizes with the tripartite resources offered in a way quite distinct from the linguistic institutions, in which case we are confronted by a solution of the problem which is legalitarian, or, to use a term from the history of art, 'classical.' On the other hand we may have a presentation which reacts against these tripartite schemes, shakes them, mixes them and offers non-conformist solutions, destined to construct a new legality, or not.

The authors are in constantly different positions in their relationship to the Planes.

The structure of *I Promessi Sposi* (*The Betrothed*) is classical because, leaving aside the problems of its lyrical, dramatic and-or epic content, which are of no interest in this context, it shows a careful distinction of the three spheres. The sphere of the 'He' is dominant, because it is inseparable from the narrative nature of the novel; the sphere of the 'You' is strongly represented in the dialogue, which is multiform in its inspiration and in the variety of spiritual level of the characters but unitary in the literary language used; the sphere of the 'I' is present each time the author in person refers to the documents he has studied or to his own responsibilities. The author absolutely *never* gives up his own vigilance and reserve to immerse himself in the world of his *narratum* and his characters. This is certainly not lyrical.

Famous examples of the first procedure, insofar as the world of the 'He' is concerned, are the exhaustive presentations of the characters as a preëxisting datum of the *narratum*: Don Abbondio (Chapter I) or Father Christopher (Chapter IV) or the Nun of Monza (Chapters IX-X) or the Cardinal (Chapter XXII).

In the world of the 'You', the dialogue between the Cardinal and Don Abbondio (Chapters XXV-XXVI) can be compared with that indeed very well balanced dialogue between the Count and the Provincial (Chapter XIX). In the world of the 'I', the paragraphs which keep the author always distinct and separate from his story: (Chapter XXVI) "even we . . ., since we have to compare only the sentences and have nothing else to fear than the criticism of our readers, even we, I repeat, feel a certain repugnance toward going on:" (Chapter XXII) "At this point in our story we can do no less than stop a while, like the traveler . . ." (before introducing the description of the Cardinal).

More specific problems arise when we deal with the world of the 'He.' In the first place there appears the relationship obtaining between the characters and the environment, between the characters and the scene, whether it is as imaginary as the characters or specific and objective, from the historical as well as the geographical point of view;

there is a style corresponding to the 'He' as a person, a historical occurrence and a geographical environment.

As constantly and equally genuine stories we can place, from the stylistic point of view, at the one extreme either a story of imaginary characters, times and places, or the *History of Europe* as seen by Benedetto Croce which unfolds about real, artistically interpreted characters, times and places. The definitions of story or imaginative historical and geographical novel[2] and of *histoire romancée* (not in the deprecatory sense of history interpreted by one individual) are nothing but pale classification inserted into a sequence.

Total adherence to the possibilities and to the limits of the linguistic institutions has its consequences; it leads to the transfiguration and universalization of the real.

Manzoni as an artist presents unsurpassably landscapes and processes of thought of people; but he universalizes them immediately, removing any reference to specific proper names and adding observations of a general nature or transferring what were the particular images and emotions of two exiles into a nostalgic flow, in which, for once, the author himself seems to participate by means of orthodox linguistic resources, as, for instance, in *Addio monti sorgenti dall'acque*.[3]

This absolute legality (Cf. Chapter VIII) is such that the text of *I Promessi Sposi* (*The Betrothed*) is an exemplary text for every sort of documentation of a collective nature, in the field of stylistic choices as well as in that of the more obvious selection of grammatical examples.

The plane of the 'He' is rather different, from this point of view, in Antonio Fogazzaro's novels. The obvious references to historical events notwithstanding, the geographical plane is dominant. The mountains of Lake Lugano, the Bre, the Bisignano, the Boglia and so forth, the villages that

2 Fubini, op. cit., p. 170.

3 See Momigliano, *Alessandro Manzoni*, third edition, Messina and Milan, 1933, pp. 223 ff.

face the shores, such as San Mamete, Albogasio, Oria, those on the mountain, such as Castello and Dasio, cannot be suppressed; but the reader would have to have been on the spot or to have a map at hand in order to place events and people in that truer framework which the topography represents for the Fogazzaro of the *Piccolo Mondo Antico*.[4]

The Sicilian Giovanni Verga, on the other hand presents an attitude and problems opposed to both Manzoni and Fogazzaro, of which latter he is a contemporary. In his novel *I Malavoglia* (*The House by the Medlar-Tree*), we cannot take exception to the critical statement that the author immerses himself in his characters or in individuals from among them. But the analysis which reveals this to us is not based on visible stylistic choices.[5] It develops in spite of the absence of positive stylistic signals with perhaps only an occasional straggling periodic sentence and one or another irrational conjunctive *that*, the scars, the symbolic wound caused by the meeting of different planes.[6]

Let us now consider a few passages from *I Malavoglia*. In the beginning, "Un tempo i Malavoglia erano stati numerosi come i sassi della strada vecchia di Trezza" ("Once the Malavoglia had been as numerous as the stones on the old road to Trezza"), there is the objective statement that the Malavoglia family had once been numerous, and that is the classic plane of the 'He.' But there is also the simile, which belongs neither to the author nor to the reader but to a distant chorus which acts on the same plane as the other actors in the story, the plane, therefore, of the 'You.' There is then the filter, the bond that reëxhumes that old simile and brings it back to us, the memory, the realm of the 'I.'

Let us now consider the end of the novel, the direct discourse of 'Ntoni: "Ora è tempo d'andarmene, perché fra

---

[4] See Russo's commentary on *Promessi Sposi*, second printing, Florence, 1954, pp. 161f.

[5] See my *Studi di stilistica*, pp. 120ff.

[6] See my article "I piani del racconto in due capitoli dei *Malavoglia*" in *Bollettino del Centro di Studi Filologici Linguistici Siciliani*, II (1954), p. 13.

poco comincerà a passar gente. Ma il primo di tutti a co-
minciar la sua giornata è stato Rocco Spatu." ("Now it is
time for me to go, because people will start to pass by in a
little while. But the first to begin his day's work was Rocco
Spatu.") These are two very different aesthetic moments,
grouped together in a single stream of thought, the objective motivation of the indirect signal of departure, the polemic bas-relief given to the character, which less than any
other ought to have been an incentive for his departure.
Only the stylistic plane of the 'I' distinguishes its two opposites, as if in a dialogue in which someone had said,
"You must leave," and another had answered, "The first one
to begin his work was someone other than you."

The function of the planes appears, instead, indirectly
toward the end of the novel, in a passage which I transcribe
here without further comment:

"Invece padron 'Ntoni aveva fatto quel viaggio lontano,
più lontano di Trieste e d'Alessandria d'Egitto, dal quale
non si ritorna più; e quando il suo nome cadeva nel discor-
so, mentre si riposavano, tirando il conto della settimana
e facendo i disegni per l'avvenire, all'ombra del nespolo e
colle scodelle fra le ginocchia, le chiacchiere morivano di
botto, che a tutti pareva d'avere il povero vecchio davanti
agli occhi, come l'avevano visto l'ultima volta che erano an-
dati a trovarlo... e il nonno li aspettava come un'anima del
purgatorio, cogli occhi alla porta, sebbene non ci vedesse
quasi, e li andava toccando, per accertarsi che erano loro, e
poi non diceva più nulla, mentre gli si vedeva in faccia che
aveva tante cose da dire, e spezzava il cuore con quella pena
che gli si leggeva in faccia e non la poteva dire."

("Instead, padron 'Ntoni had made that long voyage,
longer than to Trieste or Alexandria, in Egypt, from which
no one ever comes back; and when his name came up in
the conversation, while they were resting and figuring up
the week's accounts and making plans for the future in the
shade of the medlar-tree with their bowls between their
knees, the chatting died suddenly, for it seemed to them all

as if the poor old man were there before their eyes, just as they had seen him the last time they had gone to visit him . . . when he had waited for them like a soul in Purgatory with his eyes on the door even though he could hardly see, and had touched them to be sure that it was they, and then he had said nothing further, while it could be seen in his face that he had so many things to say, and he broke their hearts with that suffering that could be read on his face and which he couldn't express.")

The distance from *I Promessi Sposi* could not be clearer, but such a stylistic judgment does not allow of aesthetic consequences; greater or less adherence to traditional schemes is not a criterion of aesthetic judgment.

Certain contaminations or transitional phases sometimes appear more codified. Such is the case of the free indirect construction, which has no true expressive importance, but is the result of a combination of the two planes of the 'You' and the 'He.' An example is the case of the *Senatus Consultum* of the Bacchanals[7]: *Ita exdeicendum censuere:* "neiquis eorum Bacanal habuise velet . . ."

The form of the 'He' would have been an accusative subject of an infinitive: *Ita exdeicendum censuere neiquem eorum Bacanal habuise velle*. The form of 'You' would have been that of direct discourse: *Ita exdeicendum censuere: "Neiquis vestrum Bacanal habuise velit . . ."* The form adopted does not present the 'You' as forcefully as in direct discourse, but neither does it maintain the integral, compact unity of the plane of the 'He.'

But the evaluation intermediate between the domain of the 'You' and that of the 'He' appears also in forms which are less codified than the free indirect construction. Analysis of the dialogue of a novel such as Italo Svevo's *Senilità*[8]

---

[7] See the *Corpus Inscriptionum Latinarum*, I^2 No. 581, and cf. my *Storia della lingua di Roma*, second edition, Bologna, 1944, pp. 134ff.

[8] See my *Studi di stilistica*, pp. 186f.

shows that the realm of the 'You' has been superimposed laboriously with great difficulty, upon that of the 'He' as though the mind of the author had arrived at a solution which was different from the one he had originally had in mind and which was, therefore, contaminated. But this is the reconstruction of a detail which is biographical rather than aesthetic and is not an evaluation of an intersection of the motifs of the 'He' and the 'You.'

Two different planes may be found in a region which is even farther back, individual and internal. Take, for example, a page from Benedetto Croce's *Aesthetica in nuce* and one from Giovanni Gentile, not distant from one another in time of composition and dealing with the same theme, the definition of art:

"Se si prende a considerare qualsiasi poesia per determinare che cosa la faccia giudicar tale, si discernono alla prima, costanti e necessarî, due elementi: un complesso d'immagini e un sentimento che lo anima. Richiamiamo alla memoria, per esempio, un brano che si è imparato a mente nelle scuole: i versi del poema virgiliano (III, 294 sgg.) nei quali Enea racconta come egli... ...tutti questi, e gli altri particolari che tralasciamo, sono immagini di persone, di cose, di atteggiamenti, di gesti, di detti, mere immagini che non stanno come storia e critica storica, e non sono né date né apprese come tali. Ma attraverso esse tutte corre il sentimento, un sentimento che non è più del poeta che nostro, un umano sentimento di pungenti memorie, di rabbrividente orrore, di malinconia, di nostalgia, d'intenerimento, persino di qualcosa che è puerile e insieme pio, come in quella inane restaurazione delle cose perdute . . . un qualcosa d'ineffabile in termini logici e che solo la poesia, al suo modo, sa dire a pieno. Due elementi, che per altro appaiono due nella prima e astratta analisi, ma che non si potrebbero paragonare a due fili, neppure intrecciati tra loro, perché in effetto, il sentimento si è tutto convertito in immagini, in quel complesso d'immagini, ed è un sentimento contemplato e perciò risoluto e superato. Sicché la poesia non può dirsi né sentimento né immagine né somma dei due . . ."[9]

("If we start to consider any poem in order to determine what it is that makes us judge it to be poetry, we discern immediately two elements which are constant and necessary, a complex of images and a feeling which animates it. Let us recall, for example, a selection which we learnt by heart in school, the verses of Virgil's poem (III, 294 ff.) in which Aeneas relates how he . . . . . . all of these, and other details which we omit, are images of people, things, attitudes, gestures, speech, mere images which do not stand as history and historical criticism, and are neither given nor taken as such. But through all of these there runs the feeling, a feeling which is not more the poet's than ours, a human feeling of poignant memories, shivering horror, melancholy, nostalgia, tenderness, even of something which is puerile and pious at the same time, such as the inane restoration of things lost . . . something inexpressible in logical terms and which only poetry, in its own way, can say fully. Two elements which, in any case, appear as two in the first and bastrac analysis, but which could not be compared to two threads, not even if they were intertwined, because, in fact, the feeling has been wholly converted into images — into that complex of images — and is contemplated feeling, and for that reason resolved and overcome. Thus it is that poetry cannot be said to be feeling or image or the sum of the two . . .") (Benedetto Croce)

"Nessuna osservazione è forse più atta a introdurre nel concetto dell'arte, in quanto esso si distingue dal concetto della filosofia, di questa: che un sistema filosofico non esclude nulla di pensabile dal campo della propria speculazione; e c'è filosofia in quanto il reale, alla cui intelligenza mira lo spirito, è il reale assoluto, tutto ciò che si può pensare; laddove un'opera d'arte esprime sì anch'essa un mondo, ma un mondo che è il mondo dell'artista; il quale, quando dal-

[9] The passage from *Aesthetica in nuce* dates from 1928, and is reproduced in *Filosofia poesia storia*, Milano-Napoli, 1952, pp. 195f.

l'arte ritorna alla vita, sente di passare ad una realtà diversa da quella della sua fantasia. La vita vagheggiata del poeta è una vita il cui valore consiste appunto nel non inserirsi nella vita a cui mira l'uomo pratico, e che il filosofo tenta di ricostruire logicamente nel suo pensiero: nel non potervisi inserire, perchè essa è libera creazione del soggetto che si stacca dal reale, in cui il soggetto stesso si è realizzato e quasi incatenato, e si pone nella sua astratta, immediata soggettività. Quel che il Leopardi dice della *sua donna* ... ... è la situazione di ogni poeta e di ogni artista rispetto alla propria donna, e, in generale, a ogni creatura della propria fantasia."[10]

("Perhaps no observation is more apt for an introduction into the concept of art, insofar as it is to be distinguished from the concept of philosophy, than this: a philosophical system excludes nothing thinkable from the field of its own speculation, and it is philosophy insofar as the real, the understanding of which is the aim of the spirit, is the absolute real, everything that can be thought, while a work of art, indeed, also expresses a world, but a world which is the world of the artist, who, when he returns from art to life, feels that he is passing into a reality which is different from that of his imagination. The life fondly desired by the poet is a life the value of which consists precisely in not inserting itself into the life which is the aim of the practical man, and which the philosopher attempts to reconstruct logically in his thinking — in being incapable of being inserted into it, because it is a free creation of the subject and is detached from reality, in which the subject himself has become real and is enchained, as it were, and is placed in abstract, immediate subjectivity. What Leopardi says of *his lady* ... ... is the situation of every poet and of every artist with regard to his own lady, and, in general, to every creature of his own imagination.") (Giovanni Gentile)

The essential difference in the two treatments resides

---

10 The passage dates from 1916 and is reproduced here from the sixth edition of the *Teoria generale dello spirito come atto puro*, Firenze, 1959, pp. 210f.

in the fact that the world of the 'He' in Croce's view moves according to a succession of events which have presuppositions and repercussions in the group to which the author belongs, such as "If we begin," "let us recall." The examples selected from the authors are varied and presented in their own form. The arguments succeed one another before our eyes and the conclusion is not only logical, but chronological, temporal.

The world of the 'He' in the passage from Gentile, leaving to one side any aesthetic appreciation of the prose in which it is expressed, is purely logical, static, not alive. The example cited from Leopardi is quoted in full, with no personal transfiguration. If a Freudian-Germanic formulation is admissible, it corresponds to a variety of the world of the 'He' — that is to say, to a world of the 'It.'

Naturally this does not mean that Croce's stylistic plane is always that of the animate 'He,' and Gentile's inanimate, neutral.

The preliminary laying of a stylistic foundation, as it is to be seen in these planes, all of which are approximate, occasional and not binding, has a counter-figure and, so to speak, a counter-weight in the stylistic *frameworks* into which an author deliberately and organically fits his texts. It is a question of the so-called 'stylistic planes,' which favor superabundances and impose silences as though it were a question of true and proper traditions; such is the case of the poetical-literary, telegraphic and administrative stylistic traditions, born to give to each individual linguistic realization the seal of rhythm and rhyme, or that of brevity, or that of the collectivity and organicity of the hierarchical command.

Take for example the following verses from the *Inno a Satana* (*Hymn to Satan*) by Carducci

(a) Mentre sorridono   (While smile
    La terra e il sole   The land and the sun
    E si ricambiano   And are exchanged
    D'amor parole,   Words of love,

(b) A te disfrenasi	To thee is released
Il verso ardito,	The daring verse,
Te invoco, o Satana	Thee I invoke, O Satan,
Re del convito.	King of the feast.
(c) Ne la materia	In the matter
Che mai non dorme,	That never sleeps,
Re de i fenomeni,	King of phenomena,
Re de le forme.	King of forms)

In the first there is the inversion of the complement of specification (*d'amor parole* instead of *parole d'amore*) but the normal reflexive form of the verb *si ricambiano.*

In the second there is s abnormal reflexive form (*disfrenasi*) and the complement of specification *Re del Convito* in its normal arrangement. In the third there is only the anticipation of the temporal adverb in *mai non dorme* instead of the normal order *non dorme mai.* The variants belong to poetic language insofar as they are in keeping with only this atmosphere. But their presence does not constitute a language of greater poetic quality insofar as other stanzas are concerned. It is a question of a negative, static criterion, not positive and dynamic.

The aesthetic level has no link with the words and the constructions which are called 'poetic.'

Take for example the case of the following telegram from the director of a rest home:

"Mancata risposta Sestri non incognita Chiareggio lontanissima senza conforto ma Vetriolo ove stassi benissimo piena libertà medici Ramiola dovevano suggerire con mia approvazione."

("Failing answer Sestri not unknown Chiareggio very-distant without comfort but Vetriolo where one stays very-well full freedom doctors Ramiola should have suggested with my approval.")

The question concerns the fact that nothing prevented the sending of the syntactically complete text:

"Data la mancata risposta di Sestri, medici di Ramiola

74

dovevano suggerire, certi della mia approvazione, non già l'incognita di Chiareggio che è lontanissima senza conforto ma Vetriolo dove si sta benissimo in piena libertà."

("In-view-of the missing answer from Sestri, doctors of Ramiola should have suggested certain of my approval, not the unknown-one of Chiareggio which is very distant without comfort but Vetriolo where one stays very-well in full freedom.")

According to this stylistic tradition the omission of the articles and prepositions is, in telegraphic style, not only connected but almost binding, as though it were another language. From the pre-grammatical we pass to the literary-grammatical or the telegraphic-grammatical form with parallel procedures which permit reciprocal 'translations.'

Finally, take the case of a message sent by Churchill to the Minister of Labor on December 10, 1941.

"The rule I have made, which was followed in the last war and must be followed in this, was that service in the House of Commons ranks with the highest service in the State. Any member of Parliament . . . has a right to decide at his discretion whether he will fulfil that service or give some other form."[11]

The impossibility of this message based on the 'I' of the one in command is placed in proper perspective by the fact that that same day Churchill had received news which he recorded in his memoirs in a highly lyric passage in the name of the 'I' that remembers and experiences:

"I was opening my boxes on the 10th when the telephone at my bedside rang. It was the First Sea Lord. His voice sounded odd. He gave a sort of cough and gulp, and at first I could not hear quite clearly. 'Prime Minister, I have to report to you that the *Prince of Wales* and the *Repulse* have both been sunk by the Japanese - . . .' 'Are you sure it's true?' 'There is no doubt at all.' So I put the tele-

[11] Churchill, *The Second World War*, vol. III, *The Grand Alliance*, Book II, *War Comes to America*, Boston, 1951, p. 840.

phone down. I was thankful to be alone. In all the war I never received a more direct shock."[12]

The different structure of the sentences and the attempt to translate the message into short sentences and the memory into hierarchical sentences are sufficient to show how the stylistic tradition is historically justified and, within proper limits, deserves to be respected.

Such are the two introductory aspects of stylistic problems; the inclusion of the numerous planes of the story within the framework of the flexibility of the three dominant stylistic planes, the reaction of qualified stylistic traditions on the substantially homogeneous planes of the story.

[12] ibid., p. 620.

VI

REPRESENTATION AND RESTRAINT

Whatever the formula may be that results from the intersection of the various planes, each concrete linguistic realization pays the price of the immortality it has reached; it allows itself to be bound by the linguistic institutions of the community.

Just as in every community there are ever more detailed guarantees, through which one pays for security with formality, wasted time, restrictions on his freedom, so each linguistic realization imposes more restraint the more it answers to the ideals which are valid for the whole community; the more it is recalcitrant in its restraint the more it risks illegality and lack of understanding.

The linguistic system is not born of nothing, as a rational autonomous, perfect creation, but is rather the result of a long series of events, of a long wasting-away. It is a rock which has taken on its shape after long centuries of being polished by the glaciers, and it has assumed this form without setting any goal for itself, but by merely undergoing external pressure and making its own resistance felt.

The ice which has been the agent of the erosion and which has left it behind has, on the other hand, had a purpose, that of assuring itself that it can move and 'pass.' Men's purpose in transmitting their linguistic institutions to one another has been that of 'communicating' among themselves, attempting to 'pass' as easily as possible among the incrustations and irregularities of tradition. Contrary to the opinion held by M. Sansone[1] linguistic institutions *have a purpose.*

[1] See *Giornale* cit., p. 203.

But this does not mean either that they are adequate for all expressive needs, or that they are not — for they are — superabundant.[2] An expressive substance may be deformed by superabundant linguistic realizations as well as by excessively schematic and rudimentary linguistic institutions; examples are "the appreciations and the efforts of the laconic poets," a far different matter from the "brief but calm describer" Manzoni as he was called by Attilio Momigliano.[3] Analogously the blocks of ice are many and aspire to movement and the rocks are rigid and impose a form on the ice. For the same reason they "are constitutionally inadequate" for the needs of the glaciers. In no other way ought we to understand the congenital inadequacy of linguistic systems[4] and men's basic inability to speak.

Rocks and glaciers are similar and, at the same time, different; they impose the task of classification and comparison. In the same way, the linguistic systems, as history has transmitted them to us, in and out of use, are similar and different. They are comparable and translatable only if we consider not only what they agree to represent but also what they pass over in silence; the difference between a durative and a momentaneous past in the tenses of the verb is represented in the Italian system, but not in the German, while the difference between motion toward and motion away from a place denoted by the German particles *hin* and *her* is not provided for in the Italian system.

It is a question not only of the multiplicity of languages[5] but of the impossibility of any equivalence among them, the characteristic trait of linguistic systems. Juridical intuition is such that a judge is eventually able to move with a certain freedom within the overall framework of the juridical institutions of the whole world, for they are not so different from one another. Aesthetic intuition can only exist

---

[2] See my *Fondamenti della storia linguistica*, p. 17 and 65.
[3] *Studi di poesia*, p. 152.
[4] See my *Fondamenti della storia linguistica*, p. 17.
[5] Cf. Fubini, op. cit., p. 378.

through a thorough knowledge of linguistic institutions organized into systems which have no common ground.

As soon as we leave the field of aesthetics and measure the relationship between the universal value of the inspiration and the peculiarities of the linguistic community in which the inspiration has taken shape instead of the intrinsic unity of the artistic creation, we find that the labor of creation presents itself for that very reason as an immense effort of translation[6] even in its original version, even when there is no hesitation in the choice of artistic planes and these latter offer no rigidity and resistance to the expressive needs.

In different but parallel terms Croce has recognized that "poetry is always a comparison, a simile, expressing the suprasensible in the sensible, the eternal in the transient, humanity in the individual."[7]

That is to say that creation is universal and concrete and each realization, even the original, is specific and abstract. It is a *translation* from a pre-grammatical to a grammatical level, comparable to the 'reduction' of figurative intuition in music or of a literary intuition in motion-picture making.

Since, after the already described preliminary laying of foundations, the process of restraint is inevitable, less importance is to be attached to the theoretical problem of its legitimacy and its nature. Greater importance is acquired, on the other hand, by the practical problem which would distinguish among processes of restraint which are more or less inadequate for the expressive needs.

Such is the case of the successive editions of *Fermo e Lucia* and *I Promessi Sposi,* examined not in order to construct an artistic biography of Manzoni but because of the increased effectiveness and refinement of his restraints. While *Fermo e Lucia* had reached a state of symmetry and har-

[6] See my *Studi di stilistica,* p. 46, and cf. Fubini, op. cit., p. 394.
[7] See Croce's *Filosofia poesia storia,* p. 738.

mony in its syntax, the restraint was still elementary from the lexical point of view.

In the first four pages of *Fermo e Lucia*, in fact, we find passages such as the following:

> "il *fluttuamento* delle onde si cangia in un corso diretto;"
> "il doppio e diverso romor dell'acqua, la quale qui viene a rompersi in *piccioli cavalloni* sull'arena;"
> "con uno strepito *per così dire* fluviale;"
> "il lembo della riviera . . . è di nuda e grossa arena presso ai torrenti di *uliginoso* negli intervalli;"
> "tenendo quasi socchiuso il libro nella *destra mano;*"
> "giunse ad una *rivolta* della strada;"
> "dopo la *rivolta* la strada andava diritta forse un centinaio di passi;"
> "che quegli che aspettavano era *egli;*"
> "così dicendo si *svilupparono.*"[8]

In the first four examples the linguistic restraint is insufficient for the banality of the formulas which are underlined, and which are too obvious or too pretentious. In *I Promessi Sposi* they are suppressed in the process of a radical reworking.

In the fifth example the correction consists of "tenendoci dentro, per segno, l'indice della mano destra" in which the word-order is more correct. In the sixth and seventh "giunse a una voltata della stradetta . . . dopo la voltata" eliminates the horrible *rivolta*. In the eighth the revision is grammatically correct, "che l'aspettato era lui." In the ninth, the equally horrible and particularistic *svilupparono* is replaced by "in atto di partir col compagno."

The reworkings, substitutions and corrections are such that in *I Promessi Sposi* no factor of disharmony, distraction or disturbance is still felt and the reader is confronted by a text of immaculate restraint.

---

[8] Manzoni, *Fermo e Lucia*, in the Chiari-Ghisalberti edition.

The restraint is evident not, however, only in the elimination of disturbing factors. It may indicate an exhaustive application of all of the linguistic possibilities, including the price, the complications and the inconveniences of a mechanical, inadequate and superabundant system.

The most grandiose example of these types of positive restraint is the French writer Marcel Proust. If we take up again the thread of my previous statements,[9] there is no need to quote at length. Proust the rebel appears as one who has built and recognized a new legality, adding, of course, subtleties of analysis never before experienced, but giving up trying to maintain any contact or parallelism between the psychic rhythm, or the semantic tempo, and the linguistic rhythm, or syntactic tempo. Leo Spitzer has objected[19] that this separation does not derive from a new stylistic situation but from the fact that Proust passed progressively from the image of the novel to that of the 'treatise' which, as such, could be disinterested enough to describe in rapid flashes the images that were set into the well-known episodes of Albertine. I must answer Spitzer's objection by objecting that no French treatise has ever allowed itself to expand its exposition according to the solemn and river-like rhythm of the Proustian sentences. There is more distance between the episode of Albertine and a parallel one in Anatole France's *Penguin Island* than there is between the prose of *Penguin Island* in general and the psychological descriptions of a treatise such as Lucien Lévy-Bruhl's *The Primitive Mentality*.

This more violent but more unilateral restraint has, at any rate, the directness of its effectiveness in common with the better balanced restraint of Manzoni; it lights little fires in the mind of the reader, who in his turn must know how to illuminate the spaces, whether many or few, that even the wisest of restraints inevitably leaves dark.

The image of the rock now comes back as useful, and

[9] See my *Studi di stilistica*, p. 136ff.

[10] *Spettatore italiano* cit., p. 359.

for the last time. The rock, it is true, acts only passively, through its ability to resist the pressure of the ice. But, as we said earlier, it can show, if not creative, at least formative ability through the form that the blocks of ice receive from it. Thus the linguistic institutions which do not create expressive motifs but only condition them may occasionally influence them. The restraint works in the opposite direction.

As long as we Italians have to make an effort to distinguish between the two uses of the word *tempo*, chronological *time* and meteorological *weather*, until a foreign lexical system, English or Latin for example, obliges us to make the distinction, we are a block of ice which submits itself to and assumes the form imposed by the rock rather than exert pressure of its own.

If we could ask Friedrich Nietzsche whether in the title *Also sprach Zarathustra* he regarded Zarathustra as an apostle or as a prophet he would not know how to answer us. But the first Italian translator of the work had to make the decision and translated *sprach* as *parlò* because he understood him to be an apostle, while a French translator understood him to be a prophet and translated the same word as *parlait*. The author did not have to face the problem — even such an author as he was — only because the linguistic institution of the German past tense does not provide for the distinction between a durative past, like the Italian imperfect (preaching, apostolic), and a momentary past, like the Italian *passato remoto* or preterite (revelatory, prophetic).

A very beautiful confirmation of this passive restraint exerted by linguistic systems is given by Fubini himself.[11] When Foscolo needs to imagine the tree as feminine and the normal Italian lexicon resists, for *albero* is masculine, he circumvents the difficulty with the Latinizing image of the *di fiori odorata arbore amica* (*Sepolcri*, v. 39). And when Goethe wishes to present the moon as feminine, he

11 See his *Critica e poesia*, pp. 362f.

must, contrary to his own linguistic system and the masculine German substantive *Mond*, himself Latinize and use the term *Luna* in his poem *An Luna*.

In no way different is the inveterate habit of saying in Italian *Castel del Bosco* and in German *Waldburg*. But, precisely because we recognize that linguistic institutions have the ability to influence and even to urge, to instigate, beyond their ability to condition, it is necessary to emphasize that their nature is juridical and not aesthetic and has, therefore, no right to be interpreted animistically as is so often done by those who speak of the 'spirit' or 'genius' of a language; it is even less legitimate to speak of the 'spirit' or 'soul' of a nation reflected in the language.[12]

This mythology is as far from our time and from our sensitivity as that of the man who might speak to us of the 'spirit' or the 'genius' of our laws.

If we then say *nato* in the active voice and the English say *born* in the passive, the different *genii* of the two languages or of the two nations are not thereby mirrored; we rather preserve only the indirect memory of an episode: specifically, the substitution at a certain moment in the history of the Germanic languages of the image "carried full term" for that of *nato*. Today, insofar as the present *genii* of the two languages or peoples are concerned, this difference no longer has any meaning. If English has the pair of terms *betrothed* and *fiancé* where Italian has *promessi sposi* and *fidanzati*, the result is not mutual parallelism; the difference in environment, rather, stands out more clearly in that the exotic quality of the English *fiancé* reflects a halo of generic disturbance, while an air of humorous indulgence attaches to the corresponding Italian word.

If finally, to Italian *tempo* (chronological time, and weather) we oppose the neat distinction between *time* and *weather*, we again notice the present consequences of a past innovation which has eliminated the lexical independence

---

[12] See for instance Spitzer, *Linguistics*, cit., pp. 10ff., 144ff., p. 31 note 5.

of the two faces of our *tempo*. But this does not mean only that it does not reflect the *genius* of the nation; on the contrary, it means that an influence is exerted on the sensitivity of people who, because of a lexical deficiency, must make a greater effort to achieve a distinction that is obvious to speakers of English. But this difference is nothing more than a third aspect of the linguistic testimony related now to the past and now to the present, now influenced by the environment and now exerting an influence upon the environment, but never the homogeneous instrument of an organic construction, of a unitary and present mirror of the national community.

Whether it is a question of more or less rigid planes of the narrative, of the more or less strong and effective desire for restraint; in all of the examples we have considered there have been no obligatory or automatic relationships, but, rather *choices*. These choices are *acts*. They are examinations, consequences, of an expressive impulse; they do *not*, as some fear, partake of the nature of creation.[13] But in the economical-juridical world of stylistics they are on the same plane as creation in the world of grammar. The 'choice' is not even a stepping-stone for the critic, as others fear,[14] since, as can be seen from the arguments outlined above, the situation is quite the opposite; the analysis of stylistic choices presupposes a completed interpretation.

Insofar as the nature of the stylistic choice is concerned, the question of its consciousness or unconsciousness has no weight. We give no weight to the decision whereby we decide to express our joy by a warbling rather than by a poem; to those decisions we must make, if we are bilingual, whether to speak French or German, for example; or to those we must make within the framework of one language, whether we will send a telegram or a letter.

What is important, in the economical-juridical world in

13 Sansone, *Giornale* cit., p. 203.

14 Fubini, op. cit., pp. 53f.

which we are moving, is the precision of the comparison between the systems of conventions we have before us and the extent and the obligatory character of the choice which derives from it. From this point of view the choices are not always of the same kind; we go from a maximum of overwhelming self-imposition to a maximum of naturalness. The true choices are those in between.

There are those choices which impose themselves on terms which are not balanced among themselves, in which the decision imposes itself. They are the choices that are closest to the expressive world that Fubini[15] has so well brought out. When Dante, in *Paradiso*, XXXI, uses *sene*,[16] we are dealing with an old man, St. Bernard, so different from all other old men as to require a new term. The fact that Dante has recourse to the Latinism *sene* may add to the old man's venerability, but it is not a decisive element. We are, therefore, faced with a decision which involves many responsibilities, with what is almost an exercise of the will, but we are here faced with a rudimentary choice. Dante, when he finds no Italian word to satisfy him, has recourse to a Latin word. His 'find' finds no imitators (an English translator had recourse to *senior*)[17] and, from the point of view of the Italian lexical system, has no greater consequences than that which, for juridical purposes, may attach to an arrow added to serve to draw attention to part of a public notice.

At the opposite extreme is the obvious fact that when we write in Italian to a colleague whom we do not know the salutation *Egregio collega* puts us on equal but somewhat distant terms, while *Caro collega* draws us nearer, but associates a bit of breeziness and condescension with the confidential tone. Still, there always remains a minimum of responsibility in the choice, because in the Italian lexicon

15 ibid., p. 52.

16 vv. 54 and 94.

17 See Cary's translation, London and Toronto, 1908, pp. 432-433.

egregio is one thing and *caro* another; on the basis, however, of the dictionary definitions, we should not know how to behave.

In the middle zone there exists the great treasure of stylistic choices which we use continually; we choose a more powerful periodic structure rather than a weaker sentence structure, we worry, in fact, which of the two synonyms is better suited to the reader rather than which better reflects our own state of mind.[18] Stylistic choices, in their variety, allow us to define exhaustively the style of an author, that is, his position as a citizen in the linguistic community to which he belongs.

Linguistic representation culminates other than in processes of restraint and stylistic choice, in the rhythmic framework.

From the remotest times of prehistory various rhythms have followed one another, based on cadences of strong *tempi* recurring at regular intervals, alternations of musical rises and falls, alternations of long and short vowels, whether or not they are tied together by a relationship of equivalence, the lining-up of consonantal alliterative articulations, of rhymed final syllables.

We surely read Greek epic verse in a barbaric and incomprehensible way. And yet whatever rhythm it is we obtain when we read metrically:

Μῆνιν ἄειδε, θεά, Πηληϊάδεω Ἀχιλλῆος,
Ἄνδρα μοι ἔννεπε, μοῦσα, πολύτροπον, ὃς μάλα πολλὰ

harmonizes us with the well-known adventures of Achilles and Odysseus with an evocative force of which a normal reading would fall far short. And Fubini rightly recognized[19] that even meters enter into the stylistic planes of which we must be aware.

The rhythmic factor is, however, not to be immediately

---

18 On this question see my *Studi di stilistica*, pp. 23ff.

19 Fubini, op. cit., p. 269.

identified with an expressive potential. There are proses, not tied to any harmonious cadence at the end of the sentence, which are richer in poetry than well rhymed verses are. But, varying with times and ages, the search for a more emphatic rhythm has been associated, time after time, with what is ,in fact, an enrichment of expression, or with the image of a hallucinogenic drug—a source of deviation and gradual sterility of expression. Significant examples are found in Italian poetry of the eighteenth and nineteenth centuries.

The rhythmic framework is not the same in Metastasio and in Parini. The following verses are from Metastasio's *A Nice (To Nike)*:

Mancò l'antico ardore	(There) failed the ancient ardor
e son tranquillo a segno	and so I am tranquil
che in me non trova sdegno	that in me (love) does not find (such) disdain
per mascherarsi amor.	that it must mask itself.
Non cangio più color	I no longer change color
quando il tuo nome ascolto	when I listen to your name
quando ti miro in volto	when I look into your face
più non mi batte il cor.	my heart no longer beats (hard).

and the following are from Parini's *Per l'inclita Nice (For Most Noble Nike)*:

Rapido il sangue fluttua	Rapid flows the blood
ne le mie vene: invade	in my veins: it (the warmth, v. 3) invades,
acre calor le trepide	a bitter warmth, the fearful
fibre; m'arrosso; cade	fibres; I blush; it (my voice, v. 5) falls,
la voce; ed al rispondere	my voice, and in order to answer
util pensiero in van cerco	useful thought in vain I seek
e sermon.	and speech.

In Metastasio the restraint on the use of the rhythm is total, from the phonetic as well as from the syntactical point of view. In Parini it is still a matter of *septenarii* to which a hendecasyllabic verse is added. But the play of the accent on the antepenult is more varied, and the syntactical correspondence to the verse is broken. The cycle of rhythmic conformism is overcome.

A second example, less strikingly obvious and more meaningful, is to be found in the Homeric translations of Monti and Foscolo. It is always a matter of free hendecasyllables in which Monti, however, indulges the true melody while Foscolo is more careful (in the following Italian texts the stress has been indicated for the English reader):

Foscolo,
> Dìsse; e quel nàto dalla dèa rispòse.
> Nòbile erède di Laèrte, Ulìsse,
> Sàvio dei grèci consiglièr, io dèggio
> Òr con lìberi sensi, ìndi con l'òpre
> Fàrti rispòsta, ònde più mài né il vòstro
> Né l'altrùi peroràr qui non m'assèdi:
> L'uom ch'àltro dice, àltro ha nel còr, m'è in òdio
> Cóme le pòrte dell'infèrno, e intèndo
> Significarvi onestamente il vèro ...
> (He spoke; and that one-born of the goddess answered.
> Noble heir of Laertes Ulysses,
> Wise of-the Greeks counselor, I ought
> now freely and frankly, then (later) with deeds
> to make thee an answer, so that (whence) never more
>   either your
> or someone else's perorating here should besiege me:
> The man who says one thing but has something else
>   in his heart, is hateful to me
> like the gates of Hell, and I intend
> to tell you honestly the truth . . .;

Monti,
> Divìno sènno, Laerzìade Ulìsse,

Rispòse Achìlle, senza vèlo, e quàli
Il còr li dètta e proveràlli il fàtto,
M'è d'uòpo palesàr dell'àlma i sènsi,
Onde cessiàte di garrìrmi intòrno.
Òdio al pàr delle pòrte àtre di Plùto
Colùi ch'àltro ha sul làbbro, àltro nel còre:
Ma ben ìo dirò nètto il mio pensièro ...
(Divine Intelligence, Son-of-Laertes Ulysses,
Answered Achilles, without veil and such-as
the heart dictates them and the act will-bear-them-out,
I needs must make-clear of the (my) soul the feelings
so-that (whence) you should cease to shreik about me
I hate equally as much as the black gates of Pluto
Him who one-thing has on his lip(s), (and) something-
        else in his heart;
but well I will-say clear(ly) my thought ...)

Finally a reëvocation of Napoleon appears in Manzoni
and in Carducci in rather different rhythmical frameworks:
Manzoni, *Il cinque maggio* (*The Fifth of May*)
Dall'Àlpi alle Piràmidi,
Dal Manzanàrre al Rèno,
Di quel secùro il fùlmine
Tenèa diètro al balèno;
Scoppiò da Scìlla al Tànai,
Dall'ùno all'tlro mar.

...

Àhi! fòrse a tànto stràzio
Càdde lo spìrto anèlo,
E disperò; ma vàlida
Vènne una màn dal cièlo,
E in più spiràbil àere
Pietòsa il trasportò.

(From the Alps to the Pyramids
from the Manzanares to the Rhine
of that fearless-one the lightning
followed the thunder;

it burst from Scylla to Tanais
from one to the other sea.

. . .

woe! perhaps because-of so much tearing (destruction)
fell his spirit, longing,
and dispaired, but strong
came a hand from heaven,
and in(to) more breathable air,
pitying, transported him.);
and Carducci, *Per la Morte di Napoleone Eugenio* (*On the
Death of Eugene Napoleon*),

Vittòria e pàce da Sebastòpoli
Sopìan co'l ròmbo de l'àli càndide
il pìccolo: Euròpa ammiràva:
la Colònna splendèa come un fàro.

. . .

lanciàta a i tròni l'ùltima fòlgore,
dàte concòrdi lèggi tra i pòpoli,
dovèvi, o cònsol, ritràrti
fra il màre e Dìo cui tu credèvi.

(Victory and peace from Sebastopol
lulled with the rumble of white wings
the little-one: Europe admired:
the Column shone like a lighthouse

. . .

having flung at the thrones the last bolt (of lightning)
having given peaceful laws among the peoples
thou hadst, O Consul, to withdraw
between the sea and the God in-whom thou believedst).

At the opposite extreme, in D'Annunzio, the problem
of rhythm no longer appears as a more or less solid, obvious, delimiting framework. The D'Annunzian musicality
now invades the picture and precisely for this reason stands
out perhaps even more in prose, in which we can distinguish
the positive melodiousness of passages like the well-known
one from the *Trionfo della Morte* (*Triumph of Death*), and

the staticity that constitutes a kind of bridging of the gap between prose rhythm and melody. The language of the prose of the *Vergini delle Rocce* (Virgins of the Rocks) and that of the verse of the *Figlia di Iorio* (*Iorio's Daughter*) are not, from this point of view, so distant from one another. Not even by these more analytic considerations is D'Annuzio's relationship to the rhythmic possibilities of the system of the Italian literary language exhausted. And, in fact, no verse by D'Annunzio can be compared for schematic rhythms to the literary verse of Metastasio or to that of Manzoni, in respect to which D'Annunzio's remains obviously more moderate. The fact is that rhythm in D'Annunzio seeks to be a framework but becomes the substance. A flood of peripheral, marginal, extrinsic elements penetrates into the substance of the narrative and emphasizes its ornamental aspects, a kind of rhymed Baroque, without harmonies of essential curves.

Perfect mastery of the linguistic institutions, precisely because they are superabundant, may be a factor of isolation and incomprehension. After having tried to synchronize the rhythmic possibilities to the maximum degree we find suddenly that they do not come to a stop on a plane of ideal, abstract equilibrium, but that they act like a toxic agent from which it is difficult to free oneself. But this recognition is possible only because the tenuousness of the D'Annunzian expressive values has been recognized *first*.

The critical-literary conclusions are obvious. While, on the critical plane, every work of art is understandable, the identity of the individual expression and the combinations resulting from the linguistic institutions is unattainable through reading-knowing (See above) on the stylistic plane. From this point of view, man is, in the etymological sense of the word, *ineffable*.[20]

---

[20] For this matter cf. my *Profilo di storia linguistica italiana*, pp. 102f., 108f., 111, 123f., 132f. and 155.

VII

EVOCATION AND EVASION

A human society in which the individual could not express himself is unthinkable; it would not be a society. What the writer does not find in the linguistic system or in its possibilities of expansion he must make up by indirect means or by appealing to the "user of the work of art"[1] the *reader*.

And in fact the procedures of restraint described above lead to exact but not exhaustive representations. They only ilght small flames which radiate light out beyond the grammatical structures properly so called, into spaces which are dark by their very nature. It is now necessary to measure the range of these integrating illuminations, or 'processes of evocation.'

Within the linguistic system the *context* is the link between representation and evocation. It is true that we are conscious of the difference of meaning between the *is* of the two expressions *God is* and *The earth is round*.[2] But without the context the verb *is* (and the Italian *è* in the equivalent sentences *Iddio è* and *La terra è rotonda*) remains ambiguous and perhaps only a particularly energetic accentuation can evoke the notion of *existing* rather than only that of *being (something)*.

Procedures of evocation properly so called involve both the general tone, the stylistic plane as a whole, and the specific stylistic choices.

Here are some examples of procedures by which we may appeal to the collaboration of the reader, exciting his

---

[1] Spitzer, *Linguistics* cit., p. 28.

[2] Terracini, *Archivio glottologico italiano*, XXXV (1950), p. 103; cf., ibid., his remarks on Valéry, XXXVIII (1953), pp. 21f.

attention and his ability to integrate. A first distinction, already suggested by Vossler,[3] consists of the search for the *chronologically* unusual, the archaism or the neologism.

For instance Carducci in his commemoration of Garibaldi:

"Forse, tra il secolo vigesimo quinto e il vigesimo sesto, quando altre instituzioni religiose, e civili governeranno la penisola, e il popolo parlerà un'altra lingua da quella di Dante, e il vocabolo Italia suonerà come il nome sacro dell'antica tradizione della patria, forse allora, tra un popolo forte, pacifico, industre, le madri alle figlie nate libere e cresciute virtuose, e i poeti (perché allora vi saranno veramente i poeti) ai giovani uscenti dai lavori o dalle palestre nel fòro, diranno e canteranno la leggenda garibaldina così. Egli nacque da un antico dio della patria mescolatosi in amore con una fata del settentrione . . ."

("Perhaps between the twenty-fifth and the twenty-sixth century, when the peninsula will be governed by different religious and civil institutions, and the people will speak another language than that of Dante, and the word Italy will sound like the sacred name of the ancient tradition of the fatherland, perhaps then among a strong, peaceful, industrious people, mothers to their daughters, born in freedom and grown up in virtue, and poets (for then poets will there truly be) to the young men coming from their work or their play, will tell and sing the legend of Garibaldi so: He was born of an ancient god of the fatherland who had joined himself in love to a fairy from the lands of the North . . .")

It is not only the aesthetic emotion of the contrast between the giant Garibaldi and the wretched Italian society of the day which works on the reader as an expressive motif, but also the archaic tone of the epic legend that transports him beyond the centuries.

Arcobaleno (Rainbow) is a poem by Ardengo Soffici which was written almost fifty years nearer to our own time.

---

[3] Terracini, ibid., XXXVIII (1953), p. 16.

In its structure and in its stylistic planes it is separated by a wide gulf from the oration for Garibaldi. Its text is as follows:

"Ogni cosa è presente:
Come nel 1902 tu sei a Parigi in una soffitta,
Coperto da 35 centimetri quadri di cielo
Liquefatto nel vetro dell'abbaino;
La Ville t'offre ancora ogni mattina
Il bouquet fiorito dello Square de Cluny;
Dal boulevard Saint Germain, scoppiante di trams e
    d'autobus,
Arriva, la sera, a queste campagne, la voce briaca della
    giornalaia."

("Everything is present:
As in 1902 you are in Paris in a garret,
Covered by 35 square centimeters of sky
Liquefied in the glass of the window;
La Ville still offers you each morning
The flowering bouquet of the Square de Cluny,
From Boulevard Saint Germain, bursting with trolleys and
    buses,
There arrives each evening, in these country fields, the
    drunken voice of the woman newspaper-vendor.")

Rhythm and words of a journalistic, usual, modern type accentuate the disinterested sincerity and specific quality of the personal memory.

A further distinction is made by the insertion of preciosity, that is of the 'socially unusual,' by what is set off not for reasons of antiquity or modernity but simply because of its class.[4] In some of D'Annunzio's poetry (e.g. *L'otre* in the volume *Alcyone*) the preciosity of the vocabulary is even more obvious if we consider the moderation of the syntactic structure and of the rhythm.

Other procedures produce an affective shock in the reader. In irony[5] these affective resonances are the opposite

---

[4] See my *Studi di stilistica*, pp. 131f.
[5] See my *Studi di stilistica*, pp. 31 and 71ff.

of those required or suggested by the context. For example, from Baretti:

"The first chapter speaks of the institution of Arcadia and narrates, among other bagatelles, the very memorable case of a certain poet who, having heard certain other poets recite certain pastoral poems in certain meadows situated behind a certain castle, broke out in this miraculous exclamation . . .: Oh magic exclamation to which Arcadia owes its birth, precisely as a great outsized squash is born from a very little seed.' '

The attributes *very memorable, miraculous, magic,* concentrate the reader's attention on the opposite frame of mind, on a form of indirect evocation which the author believes to be more effective than direct representation.

Parallel to the ironic is the grotesque, which does not oppose intrinsic, direct resonances, but rather those which are determined by the different social levels to which words and constructions normally belong.[6] Good examples are to be found in Alessandro Tassoni's *Secchia rapita,* e.g. XI, stanzas 12, 21, 24, 26-27.

The stylistic problem consists not of defining the authors according to the categories of traditional rhetoric, but rather of measuring the relationship between their inspiration and their realization in each specific case, archaizing, imitative of the Futurists, *précieux,* ironic, grotesque, through the indirect procedures of evocation.

To the reader there can then be entrusted a more ample and almost irresponsible integration through "the rarefied atmosphere of immortal thrusts,"[7] or, more generally, silences. Such, for instance, are the silences of Ungaretti, which, like immense frames, enclose verses of few words. One of Ungaretti's most beautiful poems ought to be compared here to one of D'Annunzio's dealing with a similar subject, concerning war. In the first the reader reads one

---

[6] See my *Studi di stilistica,* pp. 53 and 72ff.

[7] Momigliano, *Studi di poesia,* p. 9.

word after another with long intervals between them and each of them transmits an endless echo. The poet is able to speak simply because he "lets nature do it." He draws away from the refined and, at the same time, ineffective techniques offered by the linguistic system. One of the most beautiful is the poem *Sono una creatura* (*I am a living being*), written on the Carso in August, 1916, fourteen lines made up of about thirty words:

"Come questa pietra	("Like this stone
del S. Michele	of St. Michael's Mount
così fredda	so cold
così dura	so hard
così prosciugata	so dried
così refrattaria	so refractary
così totalmente	so totally
disanimata	lifeless
Come questa pietra	like this stone
è il mio pianto	is my weeping
che non si vede	which is not seen.
La morte	Death's debt
si sconta	is paid
vivendo"	while we live.")

Old rhetoric, impeccable sonorousness, satisfied but not stimulating for the reader who has been served too much and is now satiated — there is a contrast in the *Preghiere dell'Avvento* (*Advent Prayers*) of D'Annunzio; for example, in the poem *Pel generalissimo*:

"Il Carso gronda
sangue inesausto nel suo petto. Tutta
la terra combattuta, arsa e distrutta,
dentro gli sorge, dentro gli sprofonda.

La malga e il picco, il botro e la laguna,
la roccia e il muro, l'argine e la fossa
vivono in lui come le vene e l'ossa,

come i disegni della sua fortuna.

Egli è la terra ed è l'assalitore.
E la forza degli uomini respira
in lui, palpita in lui, freme e s'adira,
giubila e canta in lui, combatte e muore."

                    ("The Carso drips
blood unexhausted in its chest. All
the land fought for, burnt and destroyed
rises up within him, sinks down within him.

The hut and the peak, the vale and the pond
the rock and the wall, the bank and the ditch
live in him like his veins and bones
like the designs of his luck.

He is the land and the assailer.
And the strength of the men breathes
in him, palpitates in him, shakes and rages
rejoices and sings in him, fights and dies.")

No less responsibility is entrusted to the reader when
the center of attention is fixed, no longer on silence, but on
words taken from their context. To the rushing resonant or
restful traditional phrase we come to oppose the immobility
of the word, removed from its lexical system, from its immediate semantic correspondences, and reduced to an isolated, ecstatic, sometimes fearful phantom. A beautiful poem
by Eugenio Montale is entitled *Corno inglese* (*English horn*);
Leopardian in its rhythm, Carduccian in the relationship of
its dialogue to nature, with a parenthesis which acts as a
chorus, it is modern in its similes and connected metaphors:
"il vento . . . ricorda un forte scotere di lame, l'orizzonte
di rame, le strisce di luce, il mare che scaglia a scaglia . . .
muta colore, la tromba di schiume intorte" (the wind . . .
reminds (us of) a strong shaking of metal blades, the horizon
of brass, the stripes of light, the sea which (fish-) scale by
scale changes color, the trumpet (-shell) of twisted foam).

This vision of dark sea-lights is enclosed and transferred into the poet's heart; the romantic poet would have called the whole of this "cuore deluso" (deluded heart).

We have here instead a later passage; from the understood wish 'that the wind might shake thee this evening too, O heart,' there is a jump to the wish that associates the image of an instrument with the heart, and substitutes the obvious operation of 'jarring' (*stonare*, to jar, to strike a false note, to be out of tune, out of keeping with) for the operation of shaking. The procedure is here entrusted to the attribute *scordato*, a synonym of *stonato*, but referring especially to instruments with strings, *corde*, and at the same time justifying the suffering of the heart. But the title *Corno inglese* no longer has any direct tie; it is free in its concreteness and precision. From this position it is up to the reader to build the daring and, for that matter, arbitrary bridge he needs to get to the first point where there is any lexical support — any musical instrument whatever.

Such is the process which leads to that literary language, whether of poetry or of prose, which has been called hermetic, but for this reason it ought not yet to be considered outside of the bounds of stylistic legality as it will be defined below (Chapter VIII).

We leave this definition, on the other hand, when we take into consideration the works of James Joyce. The high artistic level of his intuitions does not prevent his writing from being now outside the grammatical linguistic field and from drawing close to a kind of abstract cinematography. At this point the term *evocation* is no longer adequate.

"To evoke" by integrating the possibilities of the linguistic system into more or less showy rhythmic frameworks which weld together the thread of the expression into a greater unity, is one thing, and it is another to realize asemantic situations, which means no longer integrating the system, but *leaving* it. This second attitude is defined by the word *evasion*.

We are faced with the fact of human society in which

evolutionary or *revolutionary* tendencies prevail alternately against the forces of conservatism.

Evasion means not only negative, but also rational operations, such as illustrations, maps and diagrams and their captions. It is possible to escape from an organized system not only to turn anarchically in the void, but also to penetrate into a parallel system which is more or less external. And here once again there are interesting examples of evasions with consequences which differ as they are considered from the critical-literary or from the stylistic point of view.

Such are, for example, the novels of Antonio Fogazzaro (*Piccolo mondo antico; Piccolo mondo moderno*), and some of the poems of Giovanni Pascoli.

The critical problem reduces itself to one question. The specificity and the fragmentary character of the work, the topographical and documentary exactness fundamental to both Fogazzaro[8] and Pascoli,[9] are they sometimes successfully and sometimes unsuccessfully enriched in their communicative qualities by recourse to dialects, to the jargon of Italo-Americans, to words imitative of the song of birds? Or, in the obvious heterogeneity of the expression, is there also a clash of images, already in themselves aesthetically shabby?

When, in Chapter III of the first part of *Piccolo mondo antico,* Giacomo Puttini says,

"Basta, basta, La scusa, son qua, vegno, no La se scalda, no go fato che esprimer un dubio; ingegnere pregiatissimo, Ela conosse el mondo, mi lo go conossudo ma no lo conosso più,"
for which the standard Italian is,

"Basta, basta, Lei scusi, son qua, vengo, Lei non si scaldi, non ho fatto che esprimere un dubbio; ingegnere pregiatissimo Lei (Ella) conosce il mondo, io l'ho conosciuto ma non lo conosco più"
and the English is, as literally as possible,

---

8 See my *Studi di stilistica,* pp. 123ff.
9 ibid., pp. 213ff.

"Enough, enough, I beg your pardon, here I am, I'm coming, don't get upset, I've only expressed a doubt; most esteemed engineer, you know the world, I knew it (once) but I don't know it any more,"
it is clear that the author is leaving the system of the literary languages to enter the system of Venetian dialect. This does not come about because of a scruple or a sharpening of objectivity, as would be the case if it were really a question of an illustration with its caption. A standard English translation proves the point:

"Enough! Enough! Pray excuse me! I am quite ready! I will come! Don't get excited! I only expressed a doubt, most worshipful engineer. You know the world. So did I, at one time, but I know it no longer."[10]

The rendering *worshipful engineer* is an error, but the error is referable as much to the literary language as to the dialect of the original. From the artistic point of view, the fact that the author inserts standard forms into a dialect passage neither deforms the whole nor reduces its value. On the stylistic plane, on the other hand, we feel the lack of 'evocation' which the dialect gave to the original, accentuating the subjectivity of the character[11] but which the translator could not suggest from without; the English reader must supply the want from within by using his imagination. The evasion toward another system allowed the author to show his linguistic sociality on two different planes. It had stylistic relevance.

As I have already had occasion to show elsewhere, the proportion existing between problems of representation and those of evocation differs from one language to another.[12]

According to Leopardi Italian is a freer language than French.[13] French has resources of greater moderation but

10 English translation by Prichard-Agnetti, London, 1906, p. 42.

11 Portier, *Antonio Fogazzaro*, Paris 1937, pp. 267ff.

12 See my *Studi di stilistica*, pp. 25f.

13 See Terracini's discussions of this matter in *Archivio glottologico italiano*, XXXV (1959), p. 106, and XXXVI (1951), p. 145.

also of greater rigidity, Italian has showier but more elastic means of expression. French, as opposed to Italian, leads to evocations rather more appropriate to fill in gaps than to indicate nuances of tone.

But whatever the definitions may be that are given to the various separate languages on the basis of these procedures, the notion of representation, once it has been integrated with those of 'evocation' and 'evasion,' just defined, leads to a conclusion opposed to that of the preceding chapter. Through it, finally, in agreement with Spitzer,[14] "individuum non est ineffabile." This happens, however, *in spite* of the linguistic institutions of which he makes use.

[14] *Stilstudien* II, p. 519.

VIII

FREEDOM AND STYLISTIC LEGALITY

The problem of linguistic freedom which is thus posed is resolved affirmatively by traditional idealists. Their certainty allows even such contradictory statements as the following: "Everything in it is absolutely free, within the bounds of the conditional freedom of which we have spoken."[1]

On the other hand, Spitzer's formulations are picturesque; he sees *trees* where others see *wooden beams* in linguistic systems; he seeks *living units* where others find only *corpses*;[2] he considers language to be an outward crystallization of the "inward form",[3] rather than a primary force which crystallizes the inner form.

Neither I nor anyone else can hold, in fact, that language *always* does violence to thought.[4] But in language we must see both trees and beams, living units and corpses, a realization of a previous thought and, as well, an ability to crystallize and, for that very reason, to enchain thought.

Linguistic freedom is a strongly conditioned freedom. These truths are not attenuated by such mystical and maidenly-modest formulas as that according to which the speaker has, in a certain sense, all human experience of language.[5]

For the most authoritative and organic attempt to define linguistic freedom we are indebted to B. Terracini in his work, the polemic part of which is primarily the title *Lingua*

---

[1] Sansone, *Giornale* cit., p. 20.

[2] Spitzer, *Romanische Stil- und Literaturstudien*, I, Marburg, 1931, p. 31 (quoting Kuttner).

[3] Spitzer, *Linguistics* cit., p. 18.

[4] Sansone, *Giornale* cit., p. 201.

[5] Fubini, op. cit., p. 364.

libera e libertà linguistica (*Free Language and Linguistic Freedom*).[6] Once the principle of conditional freedom is accepted, it is obvious that an agreement is reached: language is free within the framework of the established traditions which allow us to continue to recognize it diachronically as Italian, for example, instead of French. The linguistic freedom of the speaker is maximal and total within the framework of the analogous conventions which allow us to recognize it as such synchronically.

There may exist nuances of greater optimism. To the formula, "In living speech the inadequacy disappears,"[7] I should add, "for those who are satisfied with it." To the formula, "A linguistic system is open to any spiritual form whatever,"[8] I should add, "in spite of itself." And, finally, to the "ebb and flow of actions and reactions between the individual and the language . . . produced and worked out by the exercise of linguistic freedom,"[9] I should add, "insofar as I am free."

The following formulas, even if still too rigid, deserve more general agreement: "A language is free in those of its elements which, in the . . . system of the language, are seen to be tied together by associative relationships . . . It is not free, on the other hand, wherever these relationships have the characteristics of an opposition. And, finally and conclusively, opposition means *standard*."[10]

The difference between my point of view and Terracini's is that even in associative relationships, that is to say in stylistic choices, there is freedom, but it is conditional.

I am also in agreement with him concerning the following words: "The fruit of matured linguistic freedom

[6] *Archivio glottologico italiano*, XXXV (1950), pp. 99-117; XXXVI (1951), pp. 121-152; XXXVIII (1953), pp. 1, 35, 123, 189.

[7] ibid., XXXV, p. 103.

[8] ibid., p. 105.

[9] ibid., XXXVIII, p. 35.

[10] ibid., XXXVI, p. 142.

against the limits of a free language (assuming that the speaker has made good use of his freedom — that is, that he has been understood) . . ."[11]

Freedom is conditional for the speaker through the approximate respect of the conventions which are valid for him. And thus we continue with other recognitions of the social, conditioning element: "To take a position with regard to usage is an act of linguistic freedom, of social freedom,"[12] does mean to act with individual characteristics within society, but within the framework of the laws in force. Elsewhere one speaks of "expressive tone" and even of "social" tone, of the "ductility of the speaker and hearer" which are "two aspects of the same freedom"[13] to which must be added the limiting adjective "conditional."

The "agonistic play between speaker and hearer, between the individual and his own language"[14] can, finally, be recognized without further reservations in this formulation.

Then there are formulas in which the disagreement is greater, but in large part external, formal. As opposed to stylistic choices, Terracini states that "expressivity is diffused throughout the whole system of the language" and that choice "has no meaning or resolves itself in a contradiction, since the choice is already predetermined by the structure (*testura*) of the language."[15] If we substitute *system* for *structure* we have a more radical, almost a positivistic thesis, in that it gives up attempting to distinguish between a grammatical system which *imposes* itself and an inventory-system of choices, obviously softer, gentler, which limits itself to *presenting possible choices*. Nor does the expression *sentimento linguistico*[16] — 'Sprachgefühl' —, which has been

11 ibid., XXXVIII, p. 26.

12 ibid., p. 27.

13 ibid., XXXVI, p. 124.

14 ibid., XXXVIII, p. 12.

15 ibid., XXXVI, p. 138, and XXXV, p. 106 (cf. p. 109), respectively.

16 ibid., XXXVI, p. 133.

proposed as a substitute for *system*, reflect those rigid aspects by which a system is recognized as Italian, for instance, rather than French. The *expressive tone*[17] is presented as the equivalent of Humboldt's *innere Form*. But *parole prégrammaticale* (*parola pregrammaticale*)[18] is the same thing, and more sincere, because it does not limit to tone the totality of the expression in its dialogues and in its translation into the schemes of the linguistic community in which it is realized.

The following two statements are to be resolutely rejected for the same reasons: (a) "freedom is to be identified with the very exercise of linguistic activity,"[19] because it passes over, and thereby denies, any conditioning whatever; (b) "the potential 'treasury' (*tesoro*, Lat. *thesaurus*) of the language is equivalent to the complex of experiences of the subject"[20] because the subject has not experienced free or fanciful expressions but, rather, preconstituted conventions.

These unacceptable formulas are found on the same plane as that of Ernst Cassirer, according to which "the law is nothing else than the creative standard itself of the activity of the spirit, and therefore the form itself of its freedom,"[21] which is playing with words, by which an act proper to the juridical world is made aesthetic.

Linguistic freedom, thus defined, is not limited to the recognition of sociality when it has been transferred to the economic-juridical world. It poses the problem of a 'doing' and of its limits. Together with the theory there arises the necessity of a 'policy' and the problem of its 'legality.' Once again the difference of the world of aesthetics is thrown into sharp relief, a world of absolute and pre-judicial freedom for which the notions of legality and politics have no

---

[17] ibid., XXXV, p. 111.

[18] See my *Fondamenti della storia linguistica*, pp. 8ff., and 25.

[19] ibid., pp. 15 and 116.

[20] *Archivio glottologico italiano*, XXXVI (1951), p. 133.

[21] Cassirer, *Philosophie der Sprache*, Munich-Berlin, 1933, p. 12; cf. Terracini, *Archivio glottologico italiano*, XXXV (1950), pp. 110f.

meaning. And, as in all political activities, we find, on the one hand, an instinctive defense of one's own positions and, on the other, an instinctive effort to better the old or to conquer new positions.

In the economic-juridical world there is an aspiration above all toward stability, of relationships and of units of measurement. On the basis of this human aspiration the orthography and the literary languages have been fixed, taking their inspiration, according to the situation of the different linguistic communities, now from literary and now from religious works, now from the models of the chancelleries. The American philosopher Dewey has spoken effectively of 'safety above all' as a stylistic ideal."[22]

The same tendency is to be found in the juridical world, in the strict sense, with a strong leaning toward codifications. The same is true of the economic world, which does not refuse to pay taxes but wants to know in advance 'what kind of death it is destined to die.' The same is also true of the linguistic world when not even Terracini[23] rejects the preceptistic categories of *clarity* and *propriety*, even though he calls them prudently *aggiustatezza tonale* (aptness of tone).

But the stability of prices, taxes and laws is a means, not an end. In the same way linguistic stability is a means, not an end. "The ideal of an immobile and fixed language," as Fubini has so well expressed it,[24] is not a unit of measurement, or a criterion of aesthetic evaluation according to which we should prefer legalitarian rather than rebellious authors.

Linguistic stability is a necessary means for the individual to be able, within the environment of society, to communicate with his fellows. The citizen acts within the framework of the laws in order to affirm his own personality, not to deny it, and the economic operator does the same.

But stagnant are not better than turbulent societies. The

22 Dewey; cf. Fubini, op. cit., p. 259.
23 Terracini, *Archivio glottologico italiano*, XXXVIII (1953), p. 18.
24 Fubini, op. cit., p. 124.

stagnant history of the Greek language during the Byzantine era is certainly not richer or more worthy or remembrance than the much disturbed history of Latin. A society of disciplined citizens and of homogeneously correct speakers would be sufficient cause to weep, if it were thinkable.

On the other hand, language is not only representation in such a way as to justify a canon of linguistic poverty.[25] Similarly the goodness of economic and juridical institutions is measured according to a criterion which cannot be either unilateral or rigid. Given the situation, the stylistic canon can only imitate the economic-juridical canons of the 'civic sense' which holds that the spontaneous adherence of the citizens to the customs accepted by the majority is useful. The 'civic sense' is called *discretion* when it is carried over into the field of stylistic choices, and it is that prudence which prefers to let the reader work harder rather than burden him with unusual or forced choices.

It is in these circumstances that there manifests itself the concept of pure narrativity or 'epos' in a substantial sense,[26] which is applied to texts lacking in deliberately asocial attitudes and which are, therefore, appropriate for the construction of a bridge between the critical and the stylistic canons.

On the strength of past experience an attempt is made to validate the economic-juridical canon of discretion with respect to the forces at work through a comparison with the economic parallels of free-trade and economic planning, and the juridical parallels of liberalism and conservatism. Two works of the Americans R. Hall[27] and E. Pulgram[28] represent respectively the two opposite positions, free-trade and economic planning.

People do not look at the present or the future without

---

25 Spitzer, *Linguistics* cit., p. 16f.

26 See my *Studi di stilistica*, pp. 36, 79f., and 112f.

27 Hall, *Leave Your Language Alone!*, Ithaca, 1950.

28 Pulgram, "Don't Leave Your Language Alone," *Quarterly Journal of Speech*, XXXVIII (1952), pp. 423-430.

a desire to influence, guide or correct it, in the case of language as in economics and law.

According to Leo Spitzer's diagnosis this passing-over from one to the other point of view comes about when we become aware of the figure of man lonely in the doomed modern world.[29] The consequences of this spiritual isolation do not lead, however, to generic impersonal, colorless stylistic traditions. They lead rather to evasions, which we have illustrated above in Chapter VII, evasions which do not consider the possibility of a positive doctrine.

On the other hand, modern society, even if it does inherit criticism which is not in conformity with the traditions of the past, needs, like any society, a post-revolutionary classicism, once the pre-revolutionary classicism has in fact lost its vitality. And it needs a classicism the wider at the base the more we live in a civilization of masses and an author no longer addresses himself to an élite of 180,000 Americans, but to 180,000,000 Americans, all of whom are literate and have been taught to read.

Whatever attitude we adopt it must be substantially good-natured at its beginning; we must remember the liberal principle expounded by Spitzer,[30] that every psychic distance from the standards brings linguistic distance in its wake and that every linguistic distance is an indication of psychic distance.

This problem opens the way to two different discussions. The first, primarily economic in nature, consists of asking ourselves whether the present society of the masses, with its controlled economy and with its need for planned investments, also needs a new series of guiding principles or whether, contrary to the economic parallels, free-trade still has something to say in the linguistic area.

The answer is not in doubt. The guiding principles of criticism, whether of literary creation or of criticism as

---

29 Spitzer, *Linguistics* cit., p. 22.

30 Spitzer, *Romanische Stil- und Literaturstudien*, I, pp. 4ff.

such, are not up-to-date. Even in the civilization of the masses literary creation and criticism remain an individual matter.

But, even in the economic-juridical field of stylistics, the road toward such guiding principles is barred by the fact that we cannot suppress the transition or, if you will, the descent from the individual realm of criticism into the social realm of style. If sociality, even for serious reasons, meant guiding principles, we should certainly successfully block the critical interpretation in the realm of the individual, we should reduce it to a sterile contemplation or to a confession between critic and author. But the critic, although he must look to the author, must also speak for other men. The most austere champion of the individual nature of criticism, Benedetto Croce, has recognized that criticism also has a pedagogical, an educational function.[31]

Free-trade has, therefore, a function to fulfill in matters of style, that of allowing the work of the artist to radiate outward, once it has been illuminated by the critic. On the other hand, it cannot be a question of a passive free-trade, indifferent, ready to allow anything to pass, to refuse ever to express a preference between unusual procedures of restraint or evasion in stylistic choices.

Here it is that 'free-trade' stylistics intervenes, recording facts, creating a stylistic consciousness which will allow the maximum possible number of speakers to make up their own minds concerning the peculiarities of the authors — no guiding principles and everything possible in the way of information.

The economic parallel of this problem is found in price policies. Outside complete and passive free-trade there is not only the repressive policy of fixed prices, but also the policy of criticizing and observing documented prices which have been analyzed and made public in their constituent elements.

---

[31] Croce, *Letture di poeti e riflessioni sulla teoria e la critica della poesia,* Bari, 1950, pp. 227ff.

The constituent elements of distribution costs, once made public, create the consumers' consciousness. The characteristic examples of constructions, evasions, less usual choices, when commented upon appropriately, create the consciousness of those whom, in Spitzerian terms, we shall again call here the 'consumers of the work of art.'

A price policy is not the whole policy. It touches upon the structure of society but it does not yet penetrate into the juridical structures. A stylistic policy, substantially liberal and wait-and-see, does not penetrate into the linguistic system, nor does it permit us to draw parallels with the juridical world.

The mass society in which we live is the same one which posed for itself the problem of a stylistic legality and which is now posing for itself the problem of grammatical legality. Can we admit solutions, in the stylistic and in the grammatical field, which do not derive their inspiration from the same principles? Obviously not. Those who advocate a free-trade policy in economic matters should be liberals in politics.

In any case, the exigencies of grammar are different from those of stylistics. The declaration of what was perhaps nothing more than a prudent liberalism in stylistics was justified by the necessity of keeping the way open for artistic creations and critical interpretations coming from the world of the individual.

An analogous criterion makes us hold the conviction that, in a mass society, it is necessary to keep the way open leading from the economic realm (the proper sphere of impulses) into the realm of law, which is founded essentially on certainties. These certainties must be the more valid the more numerous the society is that recognizes and makes use of those codified conventions. In the realm of grammar we cannot do without the notion of 'error' just as in the juridical realm we cannot do without the notion of 'offense.' The grammatical or orthographical uncertainties which are tolerable in a society made up of relatively few people, where

111

only a small élite is intimately bound up with the literary language are not tolerable in a mass society in which everybody has an interest in the literary language, even though for reasons which are neither literary nor aesthetic. A policy of substantial grammatical stability, a policy which is by nature conservative, is, in modern society, more than recommendable, it is necessary.

An interesting movement, promoted by an Italian scholar who is well known in America, Bruno Migliorini, is *neopurism*. Contrary to the older precepts and to purely nationalistic and racial criteria, neopurism limits itself to recommending the acceptance of new words, from whatever source, which do not run counter to the structure of the language into which the neologisms are introduced. 'Glottotechnics,' or applied linguistics, can make valuable recommendations in this matter.

The recommendation of a substantially conservative linguistic policy must not be confused with the 'reactionary' tendencies dear to many students of grammatical problems.[32] 'Reactionary' should not be understood in its polemic or deprecatory sense, but rather as equivalent to 'anti-historical.' A measure, even if modest in proportion, which does not correspond to the conditions of the time and which is, therefore, not easy to attenuate, like tax barriers around the territory of a community, is more reactionary than one which is more serious and momentarily annoying, but which it can reasonably be predicted will be carried out, like the rationing of gasoline when it is scarce. It is, for example, reactionary, in this sense, to impose on non-Florentines the pronunciations *la hasa* (with the aspirate 'h' replacing the standard 'c' of *la casa*, a pronunciation which is peculiarly Florentine and hence the object of a certain amount of imitation) and *accasa* (a spelling representative of the pronunciation, in which the initial single consonant of a word accented on the first syllable is geminated, or 'doubled,' when

---

[32] Spitzer, *Stilstudien*, II, pp. 532f., note 1.

the preceding word is one of a number of proclitic particles among which the preposition *a* figures prominently, a pronunciation which is, however, not restricted to Florence), rather than to expend effort toward instilling the habit of correct usage of the *passato remoto* into Northern Italians (who tend to use instead the present perfect and who therefore have a tense system corresponding more closely to that of French, where the *passé simple* has, in general, been relegated to a purely literary rôle and is only occasionally used in natural speech even among the educated, rather than the Italian system in which the three tenses, present perfect, imperfect and *passato remoto* have separate and distinct but interacting rôles to play, a situation which has repercussions in the usage of the Northern Italians in the written language.)

In a mass society — and among the 180,000,000 millions of Americans — it is necessary to know both how to simplify a few now sterile orthographical 'left-overs' and to require that everyone be obedient to tradition in what really matters.

Another reason against grammatical reaction is that, in our critical-linguistic experience, grammar is not an end in itself. It is a necessary and valuable prison which we must leave in order to create and interpret individually. Woe unto us if we cultivate grammatical scruples in ourselves with such zeal as to render sterile any desire to speak in a new way! Woe unto us if we should be distracted from the fundamental task, that of returning to our reading and participating in it (Cf. Chapter I), or if we should consider analyzing to be the final goal after the 'reading-knowing' and the 'knowing in order to read.' The need for an open-door policy must guide stylistic as well as grammatical policy.

Thus it is apparent how vain are both the old ideals of 'writing well' and the aesthetic formulation that it is enough to think well for the written expression thereof to be worthy of its subject. And it is again confirmed that linguistic realizations are by definition inadequate for the expression of thought; writing well is always only an approximation of thinking well.[33] It is toward this ideal of a text which will be at the same time exciting and useful for the reader that stylistic and grammatical legality tends, a legality which is no longer conceived as a static set of principles but rather as a consciousness of the forces at work, the true and only possible actual practice of that freedom which consists essentially of respect for the freedom of others.

The cycle of spatio-linguistic experiences cannot be considered closed when we have become aware of the codified standards and conventions on which the linguistic institutions are based, through that process of substitution of reading which *is* analyzing. It is closed, on the other hand, when these conventions have become second-nature to us and have been intellectually forgotten, and we are in a position to repeat our labor of reading, understanding and interpreting the *texts*. It closes in the return to the total identification of reading and knowing in the now tightly welded cycle.

Legality, thus understood, itself contributes to distinguishing stylistics from aesthetics. Stylistics, extraneous to the world of aesthetics, just as it does not refuse the preëxisting datum of aesthetics, does not preclude a return by the reader to the world of the work of art in his concrete maturity, through the catharsis of grammatical reflexion and of his discipline, which is neither definitive nor deadly.

---

[33] Against Fubini, op. cit., p. 317, who takes the opposite view.

IX

Parallel Lines

The 'I' of the reader has until now been the center of our investigation and we have been discussing the recording, through it, of experience, first with regard to the individualities of the separate texts (critical experience), then with regard to the dialogue between authors and linguistic institutions (stylistic experience) and finally with regard to the linguistic institutions in themselves (grammatical experience).

Now it is time to consider things from another point of view, no longer subjective, but objective. Stylistic experiences, the values of words, poetic motifs, seen from this new viewpoint, are *preëxistent* in relation to us and to our experiences. We must therefore be aware of these preëxisting data, arrange them in time, and, with a participation of our own which is no longer creative but only that of the observer, define them within the context of the chronological continuity or discontinuity of a history which we shall no longer call spiritual but *intellectual*.

Precisely because our individual and ceaseless effort to co-ordinate and pass from one sector to another is not successful, the image of the circle is also unsuccessful. In its place intellectual history is to be identified with the image of parallel straight lines.

It seems difficult at first sight that one should be able to arrange facts pertinent to our aesthetic activity in such a historical series. And, in fact, the usual literary history, based solely on individual authors — sometimes on the canonically "great' individual authors, ranked as such perforce because of the unavoidable variety and heterogeneity, of their several creation — do not refer to a continuity of aesthetic creations. Much less do literary histories based on genres rather than on authors, which classify, unite and separate the epic poem or the novel according to a purely external criterion, refer to aesthetics.

On the other hand, we can arrange poetic motifs in a historical series. They would be transformed into a certain number of units if we wished to present them as a continuity, but, instead, they retain their concreteness and historical precision if, each enclosed in itself, they are presented to the reader as a succession of related images and suggestions.

The didactic motive which leads Hesiod to contemplate and express poetically the succession of the farmer's days, their fecundity symbolized by the image of the lambs and of the wine, reappears in Virgil's *Georgics*.[1] It is a question of autonomous creations which have arisen in the minds of poets who are different in culture, time and sensitivity. And still, even if they do not provide a continuous line they do provide two points in an ideal succession of lights which illuminate the culture, the taste and the sensitivity of the ancients.

The technique of the *Comœdia Nova*, as it appears transplanted to Rome, views the imitation of and the contamination by Greek models as something both allowed and consciously desired. But the emotion created by Menander's characters reappears transformed, new, in those of Terence. Judgment of the creativity and responsibility of the Roman author in relation to the Greek writer will surely vary, but in a history of poetic motifs, associations possible in a play performed before both Greek and Roman audiences continue to represent a series, even though discontinuous in time. This has no influence on critical judgment which is obsessed by the romantic preoccupation with originality, "as though art," as Croce states energetically, "were not always based, in one way or another, on what has gone before."[2]

1 Boscherini, "Allusioni nelle Georgiche di Virgilio," in *Centenario del Liceo Dante di Firenze*, Florence, 1953, pp. 143ff., cf. Pasquali, *Stravaganze quarte e supreme*, Venice, 1951, pp. 11f.
2 Croce, *Filosofia poesia storia*, p. 691.

The tradition which makes it possible for verses by Alcaeus to appear regenerated in Horace extends through a longer period of time. As Giorgio Pasquali[3] has shown, it is a matter of *aemulatio* and of *zêlos* (which presuppose a knowledgeable reader), and not of *imitatio* and of *mimēsis* (which presuppose an ignorant reader).

In Italian poetry the lyrical-religious attitudes affirmed by Petrarch reappear in the lyric of the Cinquecento and in the Leopardian age, in aesthetically more or less valid forms which give proof of vitality, even if it is intermittent. Cesare De Lollis was able to speak even of a "Leopardian Petrarchism."[4] Leaving aside our reservations concerning the use of the term 'Petrarchism' in discussions of problems extraneous to style, the fact remains that the motif of nature as mother and as stepmother appears in similar form in Petrarca's poetry in sonnet CXCV:[5]

"O natura, pietosa e fera madre
onde tal possa e sì contrarie voglie
di far cose e disfar tanto leggiadre?
D'un vivo fonte ogni poder s'accoglie:
ma tu come'l consenti, o sommo Padre,
che del tuo caro dono altri ne spoglie?"

of which lines the following is Joseph Auslander's English translation:

"O Nature, mother hard and merciful,
Whence comes thy power, whence thy whims perverse.
As this that in one breath will bless and curse?
One fountain thus sustains and renders null:
Yet how couldst Thou, Lord of the Universe,
Give wings for flight — then blind the soaring gull?"

[3] Pasquali, *Orazio lirico*, Florence, 1920, pp. 7 and 119.

[4] De Lollis, *Saggi sulla forma poetica italiana dell'Ottocento*, Bari, 1929, pp. 1-33.

[5] Ibid., p. 29; English translation by J. Auslander, Longmans, Green and Co., New York, 1932, p. 195.

Leopardi's formulation is stylistically quite different but it represents a reappearance of the same poetic motif:

"Madre temuta e pianta
dal nascer già dell'animal famiglia,
Natura, illaudabil maraviglia,
che per uccider partorisci e nutri,
se danno è del mortale
immaturo perir, come il consenti
in quei capi innocenti?"

This is not Petrarchism, in the strict sense of the word, but the reappearance of a carefully defined motif due to Leopardi's own efforts. What biographical or historical-cultural reasons may have had a rôle to play in this choice is, on the other hand, something extraneous to the (intellectual) history of poetic motifs.

If we consider the poem *I Sepolcri* by Ugo Foscolo from this point of view we find that it resuscitates poetic motifs from ages much further back in the past, such as death on the battlefield or the piety of funeral rites, which come down from times as remote as those of Homer.[6]

And an author like Pascoli — who shows classicizing Alexandrine aspects at the same time as crepuscular and familiar poetry, tied only to out-of-the-way places, to the simple events of the lives of birds and emigrants — can be a source of and an occasion for the resurrection of poetic motifs from ancient Greece, for instance love and death and the immortality of poetry, threads which Pascoli took up again in modern poetry such as his *Solon*.[7]

This history, punctuated by recurring motifs, does not give us the true continuity, the tradition. Continuity and tradition in the strict sense are extraneous to the world of aesthetics. The picture which presents itself to us when we pass from creations which are closed in themselves to stylistic problems is something else again. From classical antiquity

6 Fubini, op. cit., p. 67.
7 Pasquali, *Stravaganze*, pp. 12f.

to the full bloom of the Renaissance, problems of style presented themselves to the writer in various shapes, but all dominated by a fundamental certainty, that while language is inseparable from man, man must subject both himself and it to precepts of style. The relationship between the writer and his language is rigid.

A work as fundamental as that of E. Norden on classical artistic prose[8] confirms this truth. Whether we speak of the oratorical figures of Gorgias as antithesis or plays on words (pp. 16ff., and 23ff.), or deal with the problem of the rhythm of prose (pp. 4ff.), this relationship remains rigid. In the case of Rome there is a visible passage from rigid archaic stylization to the problematic stylization of the Ciceronian age, like a passage from a spontaneous but immutable stylization to one which is varied and complex but subordinated to guiding principles.

The first novel factor we see introduced is that of the proportions between the precepts; on the one hand the tendency toward multiplying the artifices of the writer, and this is the one which goes back to Demetrius and is developed particularly in the style of oratory which is called Asianic; on the other hand there is the trend which remains more faithful to models of greater moderation, and it is the one we call Atticistic.

This double current manifests itself not only in Greece, but, during the imperial age, in Rome as well. And yet, no change, no matter how important it might be from the literary as well as the grammatical point of view, has any effect on this rigidity. The Christian revolution sees its authors divided into followers of the old style like Lactantius and followers of the new like Minucius or Tertullian. The change of rhythm, the decadence of sensitivity to quantitative distinction, the new importance of the accent transform the rhythmic procedures but do not annul them: the *clausulae* are followed first by the *cursus* and later by rhyme.

[8] Norden, *Antike Kunstprosa*, cited here from the third reprinting, Leipzig-Berlin, 1915-1918.

If one no longer speaks in the Middle Ages of Atticism and Asianism, there is discussion of a conflict between theories of the *artes* and homage to the *auctores*.[9] The only difference is that in antiquity the style which was called 'new' gradually drew further and further away from the traditional language by routes different from those of the language in common use, while in the Middle Ages the new style seeks to adapt itself to the needs of the time, as opposed to the old style which looked only to the past.

Even when the stylistic debate is simplified because Latin is no longer in current use, as it was among the humanists, still the Ciceronian ideal is accepted in an even more exclusive way, in opposition to those realizations which are not sufficiently orthodox with regard to that model.

A language, with its stylistic precepts, cannot be taken forcibly from a man even if he has quite deliberately made himself bilingual by adopting another language for ordinary use.

Bilingualism, at first unconscious, then conscious and finally deliberate,[10] while it liberates the speaker from so many difficulties with regard to his fellows, does not free him from this restrictive vision of the stylistic precept. In Bologna, Guido Faba adds his own theories on the vulgar tongue in the first half of the thirteenth century[11] to those concerning Latin of the contemporary theoreticians of that language.

Dante theorizes about the three levels of style, which differ in their precepts, Bembo formally acknowledges the final success of the vulgar tongue, showing that it is possible to develop and impose equally severe precepts for it; Plutarch, Pliny and Boccaccio wrote in different languages and times, but their dialogue with their linguistic institutions was rigid and, so to speak, prefabricated in its essential attitudes.

9 ibid., pp. 688ff.
10 See my *Profilo di storia linguistica italiana*, pp. 19-53.
11 ibid., pp. 47f.

A first development has been very clearly brought out by Spitzer.[12] From the Renaissance on, language is conceived of as autonomous with respect to man, and thus, for the first time, an instrumental interpretation takes its place alongside the ornamental interpretation. The philosophers and technical writers of antiquity were bound by these rules just as much as the purely literary writers were. The science of the Renaissance, beginning with mathematics and continuing on into the chemistry of modern time, uses a different language, and for that very reason is guilty of infractions of the canons which restricted its technical needs no less than the expressive needs of man.

The second step is taken in the eighteenth century when the right of man to separate himself from language is recognized alongside the legitimacy of the separation of the language from man. This process culminates in Italy in the so-called "language strike" (*sciopero della lingua*).[13] Not only the order of words but also their choice and even their origin, often barbaric, is removed from the control of any sort of precepts. According to Pietro Verri, "provided a writer says reasonable, interesting things, and says them in a language which can be understood by all Italians, and writes them with such art as to be read without boredom, that author should be said to be a good Italian writer."[14]

In economic terms we have passed from pedagogical paternalism and planned economy to absolute free-trade.

The rift is closed in the first half of the nineteenth century through the competitive coexistence of the two currents, the classical and the romantic, the first reduced to ancient ideals of regularity and order, the second to mirages, perhaps even more ancient, of fogginess and sentimentalism. But both of these currents are 'constitutional.' They do not place in doubt the validity and the efficacy of the linguistic

12 Spitzer, *Linguistics cit.*, pp. 21f.

13 Toffanin, *L'Arcadia*, Bologna, 1946, pp. 151ff., cf. my *Profilo*, p. 104.

14 See my *Profilo*, p. 106.

121

institutions,[15] they do not discuss what today is called the political regime, the linguistic institutions in force.

The second half of the nineteenth century is, on the other hand, characterized by the radical struggle — which is, however, not anarchistic, as it had been in the eighteenth century — against linguistic systems as such, against what until then had been accepted and recognized in their structure. The movement, born in the milieu of the figurative arts, with the French impressionists, and then extended to music through the successive works of Debussy and Ravel and Schönberg, has turned literary tradition upside down.[16]

The most recent examples of these rebellious tendencies have been discussed in the preceding chapter in connection with stylistic legality. The whole of which confirms that style is a relationship in which both the author and his society are active, in different proportions at different times.

The historical problems of stylistics are not exhausted in theories, precepts, and in their final emptying. Along with the doctrines there always exist men, and the student of styles is also a student of men, whether they are leaders or followers in a given tradition. No differently does the student of ethical-political history define the ideal currents which act on different times, but he is also a student of the men who have realized, personified and symbolized those currents.[17]

The effectiveness with which Cicero made himself leader of a tradition is not comparable with that of Manzoni; both of them were coherent and found themselves in a situation in which they had to work out new principles when the old were vacillating or were subject to attack. But the stability of the stylistic traditions of the ancient world was one thing and the agonism of the modern world, which has, of course,

[15] Fubini, op. cit., pp. 223f.

[16] See my *Civiltà del dopoguerra*, Florence, 1955, pp. 49-62.

[17] See my article "Croce storico e Croce linguista," in the issue of the journal *Letterature moderne* entitled *Omaggio a Croce*, Milan, 1953, pp. 183ff.

known how to become aware of them and to organize them into a system but encountered resistance and countercurrents, is something else.

The relationship of sociality and asociality in the authors with regard to the conventions of their time depends at one and the same time on the authors' personality and on the intrinsic solidity of the conventions of which they are making use. Tertullian is more personal and rebellious within the framework of the precepts which were still rigid in the exclusive linguistic world of his time than is Dante, who moved in a less homogeneous linguistic community with several levels in which the predominance of the precepts was intense but did not make itself felt everywhere in the same way and with the same intensity. In spite of that fact, it was possible for Dante to become the leader and point of departure of a tradition, while, on the other hand, it was not possible for Tertullian to do so. On these bases and by contrast to what cannot happen in a history of political motifs, we may align in history stylistic traditions, the authors who were pioneers of a real, new legality — Dante, for instance —, those who gave a minimum of consistency to the patrimony of stylistic choices — Petrarch and Ariosto, for example —, and those who did not co-ordinate their own individuality with the linguistic balance of the time and who proposed choices or solutions which were not destined to be received favorably — Tasso, for example.

Another distinction, considered for different reasons, now seems clear, that between the stylistics which deals with the 'style' (of an author) and that which deals with 'styles.' According to the acute and correct analysis recently emphasized by V. Santoli,[18] in dealing with these styles, including the collective values of bureaucratic and telegraphic styles, we behave as though faced with something quite external (Chapter V); but style, in the strict sense of the term, is *not* separable from the individual author. Judgments,

18 *Rivista di letterature moderne e comparate*, IX, Florence, 1956, pp. 230ff.

which are subordinated to the comprehensive vision of the linguistic institutions and of their need to be elastic and adequate, begin to have certain aspects not only of a historical 'reliving,' but also of an 'acting,' which perhaps must be called Platonic. This acting presupposes previously accepted canons.

In ethical-political history one author is attracted by rebellions and another by episodes of a primarily civic nature. There are also judgments which follow a more precise, unique lead-wire; such is the case of the *History of Europe* written by Croce and its constant thread, that of *freedom*. Thus it would be possible to write a history of stylistic tendencies and traditions, taking as a lead-wire 'reluctance' or conformism on the one hand and anticonformism on the other, not on the basis of an autonomous conviction or of one directly descended from an aesthetic conformism or anticonformism, but descended rather from a faithfulness to a stylistic tradition.

More correctly, a stylistic judgment is formulated according to different criteria in different ages and differently with regard to different authors and takes as a criterion the functionality of the moment which makes us consider a social rather than an asocial activity preferable in the interplay of opposing forces. In Italian, stylistic traditions should be viewed with conformist preferences up to the sixteenth century, until, that is, the literary language was consolidated. The attempt to restore Latin on the part of the humanists may be considered from this point to be 'reactionary.' Insofar as the 'linguistic strike' of the eighteenth century is concerned, we must underline its positive aspects in contrast to the rigidity which had set in in the stylistic traditions.[19]

Still more different, but for completely different reasons, is the history of the linguistic conventions, of the respective institutions, of the systems in which they ceaselessly find their unstable balance.

19 See my *Profilo*, pp. 74ff., 104f. and 180.

A debate concerning style and stylistic traditions implies the constancy of the linguistic system, even if it is only subjectively recognized to be such. Those whom we have quoted in our discussion of Atticism and Asianism, of *auctores* and *artes*, base their arguments on a consciousness that it is always a question of one and the same language, Greek or Latin, even though, objectively, Pliny's Latin is one thing, Tertullian's another and Boethius' something else again.

By contrast to the showiness, the obviousness of stylistic differences, the objective transformation of the structure of the Latin language is irrelevant. A history of the linguistic institutions of Latin from classical antiquity to humanism is much more *micro-* than *macro*scopic.

In other periods we find the opposite situation. Linguistic structures are transformed rapidly, like a ship on the surface of a stormy sea. In the space of a few generations ancient texts turn out to be no longer understandable. The grammatical phenomena as we observe or reconstruct them (Chapter X) loom large in the foreground. And this happens together with a parallel fact, the less literary activity there is, the less sensitivity to stylistic theories and, consequently, the less resistance of tradition in the face of these unchained forces, like a ship which must struggle against towering waves and yet has no adequate rigging.

This connection between grammatical history and the history of styles is purely external. Intrinsically the difference remains great for two reasons: in the field of styles it still depends on the *general* attitude of the writers toward the linguistic community; and the problems which arise from it in historical succession remain unitary. Grammatical problems arise singly. Each word has its own history; *egregius* little by little loses its etymological sense of '(taken) out of the herd, flock' and acquires the generic meaning of 'select'; *leukôlenos* loses its original meaning of 'having white arms' and becomes a generic epithet which associates something white with the image of the goddess Hera; these changes come about in the absence of general tendencies in the vocabulary of Latin and Greek which might dictate them. Thus, in the phonetic field, the accent changes little by little from a musical to a stress accent, the feeling for the quantity or length of the vowels weakens, the privilege of the accented syllable makes itself felt to the detriment of the final or the posttonic syllable, and the articulation of intervocalic consonants remains stable, weakens or disappears.

But precisely because it is special in the spatial sense, grammatical history is a *continuum* in time. All these novelties have both immediate and more distant consequences by means of which, it is permissible to say, everything 'remains in balance' in a linguistic system. But the unity of the history of linguistic institutions is what comes afterwards, it is a consequence of infinite actions and reactions, while in the history of styles it is a preëxisting datum which is then scattered and lost in a thousand specific, different and concrete realizations. In contrast to the *continuum* of grammatical institutions, the continuity of stylistic traditions is only approximate. In the succession of authors, stylistic traditions receive repeated baptisms, new consecrations of legitimacy.

Even from the point of view of historical judgment the difference between grammatical history and stylistic history is profound. The former resolves itself into a succession of judgments of sociality, the latter into a judgment concerned only with slow or rapid development. Value judgments are justified only in extreme cases, whether with regard to the gradual dissolution of Latin in the Western Empire or with regard to the immobility of Byzantine Greek.

We can, of course, imagine a linguistic history which would consider in order and one at a time successions both of stylistic problems and of grammatical problems. But their association is due to the external reasons which appear, for example, most clearly in my *Profilo di storia linguistica italiana (Outline of Italian Linguistic History),*[29] in which

[20] See Fubini's criticism, op. cit., pp. 488f.

stylistic problems are emphasized where the grammatical structures are stable and in which on the contrary, they are relegated to the background when the grammatical structures are in the process of transformation.

Even in the milieu of intellectual history and in spite of those circumstances which might work against it, the nature of the stylistic problems is clearly seen to be autonomous.

The bonds with criticism and literary history are all concentrated on the rigid but lasting persistence of the external schemes, as a tradition of style, for example, rather than on the instant of maturity and completion of the work of art. The image of the parallel lines is justified.

CHAPTER X

THE PEAK

The succession of circular experiences which constitute
so-called 'spiritual history' (Chapters I-VIII) has come to
rest and has found a limit in the notion of 'stylistic legality'
(Chapter VIII). In the variation of the critical, stylistic and
grammatical experiences the unit of measurement was furnished by the text, which was considered to be immutable,
certain. The parallel straight lines which correspond to the
different forms of intellectual history (Chapter IX) still
have a unit of measurement, or rather, a fundamental basis,
in the text.

But the text can also be something else, an aim. Thus
is posed the problem of its analysis, formation, and consti-
tution, through a movement backward in time, according to
the criteria and methods of a history which we shall call
'natural.'

The geometrical image which corresponds to it is that
of the *peak*, a point toward which several lines converge. This
image has also been used in the past in philosophy to sym-
bolize the life of the spirit, and has been discussed and criticized by Croce.[1] In opposition to it emphasis was laid on
the difficulty of establishing the relationships between concrete but partial defective activities, and a complete but
abstract final activity, with which we should attain not only
full freedom from the various defects but also a total detach-
ment from the world. Croce stood to gain when he substituted
for the image of the peak that of the circle, analogous to
that which was applied and of which full use was made in
the preceding pages.

The case is different when we move in nature.

[1] In 1945; see *Filosofia poesia storia*, pp. 71-74.

If we take a position where we have a panoramic view, such as from a height, we have a visual text: natural relief, vegetation, animals, men, houses. From this high point where we find ourselves, we can go back in time, looking at ever vaster reconstructions, in the fields of geology, paleobotany, paleontology, anthropology, ethnology, agrarian economics, all of which teach us how the cypress, the olive tree and the vine on the one hand, terrasses and boundaries between fields on the other, have given a definitive aspect to that panorama, within the limits set by the art of the builder and succeeding generations of architects.

The symbol of this new research is evaporating water. Rising from the mirrors of water to the heavens, it conditions the history of the ceaseless descent of the rivers from their sources to the seas.

But its movement remains different and opposite.

We have an analogous situation when we place at the top a concrete notion, like that of the text, and *want* to understand it as the goal of a long preparation. None of Croce's objections to the image of the peak is relevant any longer, the defectiveness of the activities arranged in converging lines is not a defect of nature but of chronology. In each of them there has not yet been fully realized that 'fullness of the times' which can be identified only in the finished text.

Having left the circular system in order to enter into the peak system, we leave the world of criticism and linguistics, in the strict sense of the words, to enter that of philology. This natural or philosophical history is, therefore, important, but for critical and linguistic purposes it is not intrinsic. Momigliano's attitude is irreproachable; quite beyond criticism he has not hesitated to formulate stylistic appreciations, and when he says of himself that he would never do a 'critical edition' he means that he would never 'leave the bounds of criticism.' The pharisaical protests aroused by this statement have the same weight as the protests against the tourist whose car has broken down and who can neither build nor repair an automobile.

The central problems of philology — and they are neither critical nor linguistic — have been expounded exhaustively by Giorgio Pasquali. Textual criticism is not the mechanical result of an investigation based on Lachmann's criteria, or on less, but consists of a methodical, ever varied investigation.[2] This method informs the whole tradition and is, therefore, a history which goes back in time until it draws near to the lost original. It eliminates those codices which depend clearly on other codices, without, however, accepting the general principle that the most recent must necessarily be the least trustworthy. The medieval tradition, if it is, in fact, closer to the top, rests nevertheless on a base which is relatively broad, with the inherent possibility of influencing more recent traditions as well as that of descending from multiple ancient traditions. There exist ancient variants but they do not in themselves exclude the possibility of succeeding in reaching the top, that is to say the reconstruction of the original text. Given the complexity of the framework it is obvious that we must pressuppose a whole historical-cultural preëxisting datum, and that the textual critic, far from closing himself up in his exclusive investigation, must be taught by it.

These horizons, already broad, are enlarged still further as soon as we take the author's variants into consideration. From them we must naturally exclude complete reworkings which do not annul previous versions. No matter how much we may prefer the version of *I Promessi Sposi* of 1827 to *Fermo e Lucia* and the version of *I Promessi Sposi* of 1840 to that of 1827, it is clear that this last version does not annul the artistic and philological autonomy of the preceding versions.

But, even if we eliminate these extreme cases, the author's variants present themselves in multiple forms. The *Trattatello in laude di Dante* (*Little Treatise in Praise of Dante*) must have had its origin in selections made from

---

2 Pasquali, *Storia della tradizione e critica del testo*, Florence, 1934, p. xi.

Dante's works, an anthology so to speak, done and redone at least four times by Boccaccio; three different versions are preserved.[3]

It is difficult to establish in these cases which of the reworkings ought to be considered definitive for posterity. From an abstract point of view, it should be the last one for the reader, as it was for the author. And yet Pasquali himself has shown, in dealing with Petrarch[4] and the corrections he made in his letters, that these corrections create a number of difficulties: they lessen the affective immediacy and the chronological activity to the advantage of the striven-for formal perfection or of the desired eternity — and for that very reason less personality — of the contents.

On the contrary, the corrections may have a qualitative and not a quantitative meaning, and may, therefore, justify De Robertis' statement about Leopardi, that "he is not one of those poets who ever do themselves a disservice in their correcting."[5]

As we have seen in the case of the translator, the point of view of the writer cannot be one and one alone. And just as translations may emphasize the aesthetic aspect rather than the stylistic or the grammatical aspect, so the editor in these cases can aim at chronological exactness and thus prefer what has been established as final, even if in so doing the aesthetic evaluation suffers at his hands, or he may choose with an aesthetic criterion, sacrificing the genuineness of the author's final word in the matter.

The image of a point applied to a text is just as approximate as that of the points applied to the fortresses of the old Quadrilatero, the cities of Peschiera, Verona, Mantua and Legnago. They were points when considered as parts of the whole, but in each one of these inhabited centers there was life and free space was distinguished from the built-up areas.

3 ibid., pp. 444f.
4 ibid., p. 457.
5 *Letteratura*, XXXI (1946), p. 3.

The philological point is clear only as a symbolic 'point.' Fluidity, movement and dimensions exist in what by definition ought to have no dimensions. Gianfranco Contini has underscored these problems and the unnaturalness of wishing to resolve them with the exclusive aim of fixing a canonical form; he has correctly remarked that this happens only when we see from the point of view of the author, or 'producer,' and of his activity in creating. It is the point of view of the reader or 'user' which aspires to or demands stability in the text.[6] The author's variants do not allow of only a chonological arrangement. They have also been classified according to a non-quantitative criterion in two categories: those which define a change and a gradual achievement of a definitive text by a process of refinement, the *substitutive* corrections; and those which consist of a brusque change in the expressive realizations, the *renovating* corrections.[7] In the case of the former, poetic refinement is intimately connected with stylistic refinement. In the case of the latter, the point of departure may be non-poetic or insufficiently poetic, but, quite beyond any aesthetic motivation, it may be limited to errors of grammar or to a manifest stylistic insufficiency. The substitutive corrections are of a unit, while the renovating corrections carry in themselves the risks and the difficulty of comparisons, which are inherent in new creations.

Let us consider for example the case of certain minimal corrections of a substitutive order in Manzonian texts. A passage like that from the edition of 1827, "padre, gradisca qualche cosuccia, mi dia questa prova d'amicizia" is corrected in that of 1840 to read, "padre, gradisca qualche cosa."[8] It is a question of a rectification of an affected attitude in favor of a normal attitude.

Or the triple correction of the "se tu mi vuoi rendere

6 Contini, "La critica degli scartafacci," in *Rassegna d'Italia*, III (1948), pp. 1048-1056 and 1155-1160; see especially pp. 1052f.

7 ibid., p. 1158.

8 See the Chiari-Ghisalberti edition, Milan, 1954, vol. I, p. 68, vol. II, p. 66.

un servizio" of the edition of 1820 (p. 106) to read "se tu mi vuoi fare un servigetto" in that of 1827 (p. 98); there is a greater contrast between the immense importance which Renzo attaches to the enterprise and its minimization in the eyes of his friend. But the form *servigetto* is affected. The correction in the edition of 1840 (p. 100) to read *servizietto* is purely a matter of spelling and definitively reaffirms in the formal area the process of psychological refinement.

Different, on the other hand, are the brusque corrections which, eliminating errors and exotic elements, lend an air of orthodoxy to what was heterodox in tone and geography, for example the absurd tone of the expression "Lucia fu *inconcussa* (1820, p. 109) which is corrected to read "Lucia non si lasciava smuovere" (1827, p. 100). Other example are *"soprammani* vendicati" (1827), p. 67) which becomes *"soprusi* vendicati" in the edition of 1840 (p. 69), and the "si sviluppò da essi a fatica" of the edition of 1827 (p. 67), which becomes "si liberò da essi a fatica" in that of 1840 (p. 69), and, finally, "la modestia un po' guerriera delle *foresi"* (1827, p. 36) the last word of which is changed to read *contadine* in the edition of 1840 (p. 38). We cannot say that poetic creativity has changed, while, on the other hand, it is certain that the aesthetic reactions of the 'users' are very strong, as though they were passing from a text written in a foreign tongue to one written in their own language.

If we take up again the geometrical image, we find that we already have in the symbolic point of the peak the trace of lines converging from different regions, just as in the symbolic point which represents a city on a map we must imagine the beginnings of the great highways which come from different directions.

It is now a question of defining those directions and points from which these ideal and extreme lines converge on the point of the peak.

According to the first of these two lines the question is posed whether, before a text with its possible variants, there may have existed true and proper partial drafts, back beyond which we must go in time, leaving the confines of textual criticism, in order to take into consideration those texts and models which may have been the source of the inspiration.

The discussion of the presumed antecedents of *Fermo e Lucia*, which is excellent even though it leads to negative results, is intimately connected with the first of these points of view.[9] It follows the biographical reconstruction of the work — first, for example, the rough sketching of the principal characters, then the introduction of the historical element which presupposes research and historical judgments, some of which are even extraneous to the novel — with proof that it was *not* written as a finished novel, as M. Barbi had maintained.[10] But the distant inspiration, the tradition which from a distance may have influenced it, is defined in quite another way. If we do not go back to a cultural atmosphere or to poetic motifs comparable to the linguistic notion of an age of proto-Romance speech, it is clear that at the base of *I Promessi Sposi* there are concrete 'sources' which the artistic inspiration has transfigured; for example there is the insertion into an artistic inspiration of a Christian sentiment which, recent in Manzoni's intellectual experience, has suggested itself again and again throughout the centuries to generations of poets and prose writers, and no less important is the insertion of reflexions on the progress of history which Manzoni integrated into his art without indulging in approximations and deformations. Just as the distant origins of its language are to be found in the world of Vulgar Latin, so the distant origins of *I Promessi Sposi* are to be found in an art which openly accepts two non-formal elements, the Christian tradition, and respect for historical truth.

The classic work on the direction of the distant 'sources'

9 ibid., pp. 753ff.

10 ibid., pp. 755f.

is that by Rajna, *Le fonti dell'Orlando Furioso.*[11] In this work it is clearly established that two things are clearly given, the direct dependence of Boiardo's *Orlando Innamorato*, the disordered inklings which, so to speak, Ariosto accepted in spite of himself from the double tradition of the material of the Carolingian and of the Breton epic cycles, and, secondly, the permissive presence of motifs which derive their inspiration from works of classical antiquity, from the *Metamorphoses* to the *Argonauticae*, the sources of their formal perfection.

The weakness of this monumental work is not to be found so much in the importance given to the sources as in the omission of a fundamental distinction. The 'inklings' which give rise to a poetic motif such as the relationships between the figures of Angelica and Sacripante or to Orca or Orlando's madness are one thing and the episodes which are not regenerated but only readapted are something else.

We cannot compare objectively the meeting between Rinaldo and Sacripante in Book I of the *Orlando Innamorato* and that of the same two characters in Book II of the *Orlando Furioso*. It is not yet a question of an artistic source, while such is indeed the case, on the other hand, of Rodomonte, a widely inclusive poetic creation which is not spread out in episodes such as those of the abduction of Frontino, the duel with Mandricardo or the meeting between Isabella and the hermit.

Even though with this research we easily bridge a gap of centuries of literary history, there remains some dissatisfaction. The grafting of Christian morality and historiographical objectivity onto a great artistic inspiration does not lead us automatically to the reality of *I Promessi Sposi*, precisely as we do not arrive directly at the stage of language represented in the work from the reconstructed phonetic and morphological system of proto-Romance.

Having abandoned the philological fixing of the text

---

[11] Rajna, *Le fonti dell'Orlando Furioso*, Florence, 1876, second edition 1900.

and of the classification, even the qualitative classification of the author's variants, we reconstruct a history which is no longer exclusively the history of that text but is not yet the traditional linguistic comparison.

This intermediate history is a reconstruction of *stylistic* preëxisting data which permit us to pursue two objectives, namely to recognize the formation of the text insofar as it did not depend on the author's will, and the formation of the author independently of this specific text.

The former consists of placing the sources properly within the broad outlines of a scheme. The "Milanese story-history [storia] of the seventeenth century" together with all its poetic elements takes the shape not of a poem, a *novella* or a play, but of a "novel" and of that variety of the novel in which historical reality supplies an outline and a framework for the imaginative material.

Sir Walter Scott, with his historical novels which begin to appear with *Waverley* in 1814, is neither an artistic nor a historical nor a philosophical, but a *stylistic* source for Manzoni; he supplied a model for the preliminary organization of Manzoni's poetic material. To go back to Sir Walter Scott means to go back beyond the various reworkings carried out by Manzoni toward a preëxisting datum which explains the structure of these latter. To stop this side of that religious and historical inspiration which is the true source of *I Promessi Sposi*, but to go back beyond the philological formation of the work means to delineate an area or a phase of research to which properly belongs the name *stylistics*.

Analogously when we discuss the title of the *Orlando Furioso*[12] or the ways in which the cantos end[13] or the external characteristics of the poem of chivalry or of its octaves, we do not carry out a literary investigation of the sources as inklings of poetic inspiration going back to

[12] ibid., pp. 66ff.
[13] ibid., pp. 96ff.

Carolingian or Arthurian sources nor, for that matter, do we consider Ariosto's attitude in the successive editions of the *Furioso*. We are, rather, carrying out a stylistic investigation of the way in which the 'material' is distributed within the framework. If Sir Walter Scott is exclusively a stylistic model for Manzoni, Boiardo is partly a source, but above all a stylistic model.

The weaknesses we have recognized in Rajna's famous work are not peculiar to it. They are the weaknesses of all traditional criticism based on the external (stylistic) criterion of the literary genres which have been illegitimately turned to uses which in themselves are quite legitimate (aesthetic). From Aristotle to Hippolyte Taine there is, from this point of view, no fundamental antithesis, while there certainly is such a fundamental antithesis dividing Aristotle from the cosmogony and physics of the nineteenth century. When Taine speaks of the three *ensembles* — the complex of an author's works, his school and atmosphere in which he worked — from which Greek tragedy as well as Gothic architecture descend, he suggests to us concepts which are not incorrect, but terribly partial and unilateral. Not mistaken, but terribly unilateral is his own classic formulation: "Nous arrivons donc à poser cette règle que pour comprendre une œuvre d'art, un artiste, un groupe d'artistes, il faut se représenter avec exactitude l'état général de l'esprit et des mœurs du temps auquel ils appartenaient. Là se trouve l'explication dernière; là réside la cause primitive qui détermine le reste."[14]

The constructions of modern writers, Kayser[15] and Petersen,[16] the very informing principle of the manual of Wellek and Warren,[17] ought not to be condemned too hastily, as usually happens with idealistic critics, but should rather

[14] Taine, *Philosophie de l'art*, Paris, 1865, p. 13.

[15] Kayser, *Das sprachliche Kunstwerk*, fourth edition, Bern, 1956.

[16] Petersen, *Die Wissenschaft von der Dichtung*, I, Berlin, 1939.

[17] Wellek and Warren, *Theory of Literature*, London, 1954.

be reduced to proper proportion, enclosed within appropriate limits. They have nothing to do with aesthetic criticism, literary criticism, judgments of style or the history of styles, but are limited to defining in different eras that 'propprison' which allows or imposes a particular structure on literary creations. Within the area of the three great figures — the circle, the parallel lines, the peak — literary genres are clearly separate things only in the last of the three. And they do not account for all of it, but only for that part which leads from the work of art back to its distant sources. And in this reconstruction the genres concern only the intermediate phase, which is no longer a source and not yet a new creation.

The second objective refers to the modifications introduced by Manzoni, for example, and listed above in our discussion of the definition of stylistics. They ought to be studied not simply in themselves, but in relation to Manzoni. If the deletions, such as those practiced upon the text in the part referring to the nun of Monza, prove that there was a development in Manzoni's aesthetic sensitivity, the modifications we have studied above allow us to reconstruct the development of his style. Insofar as the relationship between Manzoni as a poet and the society he lived in is concerned, leaving the world of the *foresi* (archaic word for 'peasant') and passing over into the world of the *contadini* (normal word for 'peasant') is a detail of Manzoni's biography insofar as it bears on his ability to communicate with his contemporaries, and it is quite outside of the text of *I Promessi Sposi* as a unit sealed up within itself.

There derives from this the justification and, at the same time, the exact delimitation of so-called stylistic criticism, which would be better labeled formal. It is unwise to force comparisons between this kind of criticism and aesthetic or linguistic criticism. Fubini[18] is right, of course, when he states that analysis of the variants does not weaken

18 Fubini, op. cit., p. 77.

139

"the preliminary need for a first, unitary apprehension of the poetic work." But if the philological critic aims to reconstruct the expressive formulas, one by one, in their genesis, succession and variants, as the textual critic puts together a text through special work, we must state that his criticism is something else. We cannot oblige him to reverse the terminal points of the problem.

For the same reason, and in the light of what has been said from the beginning, it is not correct to say that linguistic criticism — that is, stylistic analysis — "is confused with stylistic criticism and, in any case, is only one particular aspect of it."[19] Although the object of study is the same as that of aesthetic and formal criticism, 'linguistic' criticism is a continuation, an outgrowth of the former, and has a point of view which is antithetical to that of the latter, which it ceaselessly meets without, however, conflict or interference. So-called stylistic criticism, therefore, finds itself opposed to the stylistic *momenta* which it analyzes for purposes of writing the biography of either the author or his work, and accepts its limitedness, which derives from the fact that it does not deal with the work of art from an all-inclusive point of view. This is the condition which is parallel to that of criticism based on the genesis of the work of art. It is a criticism which is specialized in 'reading in order to know,' not that criticism, which has no accompanying adjective, which is, in its turn, the indispensable condition for a *stylistics* unqualified by an adjective. We may speak, therefore, of a criticism of preëxisting data and of a connected stylistic analysis of the preëxisting data, and not of judgment, whether aesthetic or stylistic, of the work of art.

On the rigorously philological level to which the point of any Italian text belongs, another line leads to a level some fifteen centuries distant in time from us, which is exclusively a matter of comparative linguistics. The whole intermediate zone constitutes a sort of void, or at least a nameless area.

---

[19] ibid., p. 113.

Through reconstruction and the methods of comparative grammar, we arrive on the one hand at the point of departure for proto-Romance, Vulgar Latin. The ideal line which ends in the very personal literary language of Manzoni has its other point in the anonymous level of Vulgar Latin. It could, if we so desired, be prolonged even further back in time, back to the world of reconstructed Indo-European.

The famous sentence, "Quel ramo del lago di Como che volge a mezzogiorno," — the first sentence of *I Promessi Sposi* — carried back by reconstruction to the proto-Romance phase, would include the following items in the following order: *eccu', illu, ramu, de, illu, lacu, de, Como, qui, volvit, ad, mediu, diurnu,* points of departure at which we arrive by following back an unbroken thread. Occasionally the thread is not straight, for to get to *lago* from *lacu* we must leave Tuscany, first going north and then south again to Rome, while we reconstruct *mediu* and *diurnu,* both of which contain the group *diu,* from two different modern bases, *mezzo,* with its *zz,* and *giorno,* with its *g.*

Just as in the search for sources, the problems of linguistic reconstruction pass through a nameless zone which is also stylistic in nature.

A few examples prove the existence of stylistic traditions, which antedate the authors, but which sometimes survive in the form of unharmonious remains in their works. We draw our first example from the Greek epic. No one doubts that Homer transmitted to us an epic narrative, or, in stylistic terms, that he moved on the level of the 'He.' (See above) And yet this crystallization of the 'He' represents a point of arrival, not for Homer, but for the linguistic tradition which he reflects.

In the normal narrative the introduction of direct discourse ought to be indicated by a momentaneous past (aorist). To take an example from a specific work, the thirteenth

[20] *Homer's Iliad,* London, 1884.

book of the Iliad in Chapman's[20] English translation shows the following: *said, spake, inspired, moved, replied, answered, insulted, exclaimed.* Monti's Italian translation almost always shows the same situation, occasionally, however, with the historical present *risponde*: *rispose, gridò, replicò, disse, soggiunse, riprese*; the imperfect appears twice: *guidava, dicea.* In the Homeric text the imperfects are in the majority: *ephē, phato, ēudā, ēmeíbeto,* as compared to *eîpe, ēuse, epeúksato, phónēsen.*

It is likely that already in Homer's time there was no longer any difference between them and that they all served simply to introduce direct discourse, and always on the level of the 'He.' But the persistence of the imperfects shows us that in an earlier time direct discourse had an autonomy of its own and that it was placed on another level, accompanied by a *didascalia* in which the imperfect served not to introduce and to give way to direct discourse but rather to accompany it at a distance on a parallel level. Direct discourse still belonged to the level of the 'You,' and the imperfect was its protocol, separate but permanent.

All of this does not pertain to Homer, does not explain Homer, but neither does it belong to comparative Indo-European linguistics. It is a *stylistic* preëxisting datum for Homeric language.

In the Twelve Tables, which show a technical language of the law, the paratactic structure should be opposed not only to that of the following centuries, which was so different. When we find ourselves confronted by a phrase like *si in ius vocat ito*[21] the conjunction *si* either already has the subordinating value of classical times, and then it would belong to a period much more recent than the fifth century, or it has, as it ought to have, correlative value, and then it presupposes a phase even more archaic than that with which we are dealing. The fictitious correlation on our level is only the development of a more archaic correlation, founded

21 See my *Storia della lingua di Roma,* p. 95f.

on two different levels of the 'You' rather than only on that of the 'He.' This makes us think of a formulaic dialogue, "si in ius vocat?" "ito," as though it were some kind of catechism.

This phase, more archaic than that of the Twelve Tables, is not pushed back into Indo-European antiquity simply for that reason. Nor does it transfer the language of the Twelve Tables out of its own world into that of phonetics and morphology. It is transferred only onto a level which is neither aesthetic nor grammatical, that is to say that it is transferred onto a stylistic level, an intermediate level, to be considered, in time, as a preëxisting datum for that maturation and crystallization which we find documented in the fifth century.

The third — and modern— example grows out of the interesting discussion which has arisen primarily as the result of Fubini's work[22] in connection with a judgment of the Swiss scholar Jenni concerning Alfieri. In comparison with the vivacity, tempered by a classical language, which has traditionally been recognized as characteristic of his *Vita*, and which I have also recognized,[23] Jenni has brought out a heterogeneous, irregular aspect, tied rather to the disordered heredity of the eighteenth century.

It is a question here, however, no longer of stylistic levels, but of stylistic *traditions* which, in the works of an author, are not subjected to a single discipline. It is legitimate to discover that there survive two different traditions in the preëxisting datum of the prose of the *Vita*, or rather, that side by side with a positive tradition of classicism there survives another of insensitivity or indifference.

The negative side of the discussion consists of the confusion of the stylistic with the aesthetic point of view. Jenni's work deserves stylistic recognition, but should not lead to aesthetic conclusions; Fubini's criticism is justified on the aesthetic level, but the unity of the aesthetic interpretation

[22] Fubini, op. cit., p. 123.

should not be projected into the obvious stylistic asymmetries and annul them.

Stylistic homogeneity is not yet a canon to be imposed on aesthetics and to be deduced from aesthetics.

Other examples, on the other hand, are so extreme as no longer to constitute a projection of the author toward a more or less distant preëxisting datum, but, rather, as to provoke a break with respect to the author, who, for this reason, is refused or split up into two distinct personalities.

One of the most obvious examples is given by the events of Aeschylus' *Prometheus Bound*. At the beginning of the century J. Wackernagel[24] thought that he could lend comfort to the doubts concerning its paternity, by using a stylistical-grammatical criterion such as the use of the so-called resultative perfect, that perfect which directs attention toward an object without direct consequences for the subject. Examples of this perfect are rather rare in the other works of Aeschylus. The stylistic imprint which it gives to the *Prometheus* was supposed to be analogous to that which would be apparent in the frequent use of the *passato remoto* by a northern Italian writer, who, because of his dialect background, would normally have to learn to handle the *passato remoto* as a 'foreign' tense, which corresponded to nothing in his own background.

But the most grandiose application of these criteria is occasioned by the Homeric problem. Homeric language, on the one hand, constitutes the basis of Greek historical grammar, but after having helped to create that grammar, it becomes its victim. Greek historical grammar has proved the lack of linguistic unity in Homer; the historical-linguistic view has shown the heterogeneity of the stylistic relationship between Homer and the community of his time. The

23 See my *Profilo*, p. 111.

24 Wackernagel, "Über die sprachlichen Eigenarten des Prometheus," in *Verhandlungen der 46. Philologen-Versammlung in Strassburg*, Leipzig, 1901; *Studien zum griechischen Perfekt*, Göttingen, 1904, pp. 11, 14 and 17. Cf. Peretti, *Studi italiani di filologia classica*, N.S. V (1927), pp. 205-207.

polemic against the existence of unity is fed by stylistic facts of considerable weight.[25]

Precisely because it is autonomous, stylistics must be neither underestimated nor bloated up out of size and shape. Its exaltation by Dámaso Alonso[26] should be interpreted with certain restrictions. "Stylistics is the only possible science of literature" — a statement which is acceptable if we accent the word 'science.' It is no longer acceptable if we place the accent on 'literature'; because the latter allows, or rather requires the activity of interpretation, which, in order to be individual, cannot be stylistic. And nonetheless, even for this third stylistics, we cannot deny ties with criticism, but they exist only with that criticism the aim of which is to reconstruct the formation, that is to say the biography, of the text, within the framework of the first vague distinctions made among the genres, and of connected schemes.

<hr/>

[25] See, for example, the technique applied by B. Marzullo in his *Problema omerico*, Florence, 1952.

[26] D. Alonso, *Poesía española, Ensayo de método y límites estilítiscos*, second edition, Madrid, 1952, pp. 482f. Cf. Schiaffini in Spitzer, *Critica stilistica* cit., p. 3.

CONCLUSION

In the foregoing pages stylistics has appeared, in relation to literary criticism, in three different lights; in chapters I-VIII, within the framework of the spiritual experiences of the reader, in IX within the framework of the formation and development of the literary traditions, and in X within the framework of a reconstruction, going back into time, of the stylistic preëxisting data of the literary work. In the three cases the fundamental prerequisite of its autonomy remains constant: it is respectively (a) the science of style as it results from the relationship existing between the individual and his linguistic community, (b) the science of styles insofar as they become firmly established traditions and models, and (c) the science of the stylistic preëxisting data, from which the individual and definitive realizations emerge.

The notion of "relationship" between the individual and his society — now realized, now crystallized, now in the process of being constituted — gives to these different aspects of stylistics a strong unity of substance. But, this strong characterization notwithstanding, in none of the three panoramas is stylistics excluded from the other three activities — criticism which is now presupposed, now parallel, now prepared, but never unknown; grammar, now prepared, now parallel, now presupposed.

In such a state of affairs we are assailed by a doubt. Can we really find a sound basis for such an ample discussion of unity which is variety, and variety which is unity of experiences and observations which are (successively or parallelly) critical, stylistic and grammatical? Do we not perhaps fall into the trap of using ready-made phrases, ambivalent formulations, the often badly treated plays on words, or, according to the best of hypotheses, a purely classificatory or formal exercise?

The encouragement needed to render these statements valid and to keep the problem vitally alive comes from precisely that author who has fought hardest to uphold the view of unity not only in stylistic matters, but in the whole area of linguistics, stylistics and grammar, Leo Spittzer. In spite of the unity which he diagrammed and proclaimed, he bears witness to the variety — and for that very reason to the vitality — of stylistics internally and in its relations with the manifestations of allied disciplines.

He has spoken, for example, of my two stylistics,[1] praising the one and deprecating the other. In reality the praise given to the literary aspects of my stylistic investigations leads to the dissolution of stylistics in literary criticism, and it is not easy to see how, after this dissolution, he can still be considered a champion of stylistic studies. The second stylistics remains alive, at least, after his analysis, but at the price of being carried over onto the level of pedagogical grammar, quite outside linguistic science. The preceding pages show how the notion of 'stylistics' has an autonomy of its own, even though it remains inseparably linked to criticism as well as to grammar.

Spitzer then presented the double aspect of his stylistics in the anthology on stylistic criticism and the history of speech[2] in which he maintains on the one hand that stylistics and criticism constitute a kind of indissoluble pair, and extracts, on the other hand, from grammar those problems of semantics and historical lexicology which, through history, are rescued from the hands of the grammatical pedagogue. In spite of this insight, the division unconsciously admitted by Spitzer is tripartite. The character of the first three studies, clearly concerned with stylistics and method, is one thing, that of the remaining essays of the same first part

[1] *Spettatore italiano*, VIII (1955), pp. 356ff.

[2] *Critica stilistica e storia del linguaggio*, edited by A. Schiaffini, Bari, 1954; cf. my article in *Ponte*, XII (1956), pp. 113-115.

which are devoted to texts of La Fontaine, Racine, and Voltaire and are of a critical nature is something else.
Finally, Spitzer has certainly *not* refuted the naturalistic method of reconstruction. His so-called 'philological circle' (see above) is in reality only apparently a completely circular movement returning to its point of origin; in the first part it is identical to the naturalistic procedure of reconstruction. By placing the two movements on the same level it diminishes the historical and 'reviving' dignity of the so-called 'return.'

A second naturalistic aspect which survives in Spitzer is his devotion to the 'detail'[3] even if what brings it to a conclusion is not the sum of many small things, but the intervention of a subjective click.[4]

A third example is to be found in the term 'psychogram'[5] which seems more appropriate to a precisely defined collective situation than to a critical evaluation.

That the naturalistic frame of reference, from bottom to top, no matter how diligent and totalitarian it may be in the collection of facts, does not allow either total unity or a *vue d'ensemble*, is shown by one of Spitzer's most beautiful analyses, that of the *Récit de Théramène* in Racine's *Phèdre*. In what Spitzer calls his *macro*scopical analysis, *micro*scopical analysis is foreseen with optimum results.[6]

If, therefore, in his practice Spitzer recognizes the importance due to naturalistic procedures, even if it means leaving their confines at the proper moment, nothing constrains him to be so polemical in theory against the sociologism, normativism and phonetism of late nineteenth-century linguistics.[7] Precisely because grammar, stylistics and criticism operate within the same domain and all three can displace the center of attention appropriately — to the sub-

3 Spitzer, *Linguistics*, cit., p. 24.
4 ibid., pp. 6-7.
5 ibid., p. 15.
6 ibid., p. 91.
7 ibid., p. 2-3.

149

ject, the object and the preëxisting datum of the object, respectively — nothing can be shorn of value or excluded at the very beginning except for autobiographical reasons. The continuity and maintenance of an escalator are technical problems, quite independent of problems of tourism or aesthetics which are relevant only in certain respects.

Autonomy and insertion, unity and variety, thus delineated within the notion of stylistics, are neither conscious efforts of the will nor plays on words, nor, much less, eclectic attempts. They are the faithful reproductions of a ceaseless movement by means of which the stylistic consideration of the facts of language is sometimes restrained in the genuineness of studies of relationships, and sometimes gravitates toward the individual aspect proper to criticism, or toward the collective aspect which is proper to grammar. In precisely the same way, in man's dialogue with society sometimes there is equilibrium and sometimes greater relief is given to the rôle of the speaker or to that of the hearer.

The position which distinguishes and recognizes on the theoretical level the multiform ties among the institutions, traditions and creations of reality, conforms to historical reality and is, therefore, more correct. The position, on the other hand, which confuses them on the theoretical level and must, in spite of itself, distinguish the multiform aspects of the real on the practical level adheres much less closely to historical reality and is, therefore, less correct.

For that reason, the scholar who defines an author's style in terms of the society of his times, who follows it as it evolves and hardens into a model and goes back in time to reconstruct its formation, does not make three different professions of faith. He only looks at things from different points of view. He does not contradict himself, he does not strip himself of authority, if he seeks support sometimes rather in those theoretical experiences which aim at rationalizing by *filtering* what we already know, and sometimes in those practical experiences which aim at constructing in an orderly way by *adding up* what we aspire to know.